Praise for
Giant Killers

"I love Dennis—his words, his music, his story. My hunch is, if you don't already, you will soon."
—MAX LUCADO

"Fighting great giants demands great courage. Dennis Jernigan is a man of tremendous courage who will help you learn to fight the giants in your life."
—STEVE FARRAR, author of *Point Man* and *Finishing Strong*

"Dennis Jernigan knows from experience what it means to confront and defeat the giants most of us would rather not face. Now, having lived out these principles in his own life, he wants to help others free themselves from the besetting sin and paralyzing guilt that keep them from realizing their potential in Christ. Liberated and equipped with the truths they'll discover in this resource, readers will be empowered to go forth and conquer the giants that the world too often glorifies."
—MIKE HALEY, Director of Gender Issues for Focus on
the Family and author of *101 Frequently Asked Questions
About Homosexuality*

"There is no one better equipped to minister to those needing hope in slaying the giants in their lives than...Dennis Jernigan. You will find this book honest and vulnerable as Dennis shares his heart with you. Dennis is the real deal!"
—DR. GARY ROSBERG, author of *Divorce-Proof Your
Marriage* and cohost of *America's Family
Coaches...LIVE!* radio program

"In *Giant Killers,* Dennis is revealing and sensitive, yet realistic and tough in his approach to waging war on the giants of sin in our lives. This book is useful for anyone in the midst of a struggle who wants keys to deliverance and growth. Read and reread this text! Your life will be changed, your mind eased, and your spirit strengthened."
—NICOLE JOHNSON BAKER, Miss America 1999,
television host, and author

"Dennis Jernigan draws upon his own experience to show how we can overcome the real giants in our lives. He reminds us that freedom is knowing and walking in God's will. Dennis also exposes us to the tools we need to walk in that freedom."
—TOM COBURN, MD, U.S. senator, Oklahoma

"This book is absolutely a life-changing tool! We know that God will bless Dennis's transparency and his willingness to expose the Enemy's lies in his own past, bringing truth and hope to the hopeless, with the testimony of God's grace and power!… Dennis, his precious family, and this amazing book are living proof that God heals, restores, and gives us victory over every 'giant' in our lives through Jesus Christ!"
—NATHAN AND CHRISTY NOCKELS, Watermark

GIANT
KILLERS

GIANT
KILLERS

CRUSHING STRONGHOLDS, SECURING FREEDOM IN YOUR LIFE

Dennis Jernigan

WaterBrook
PRESS

GIANT KILLERS
PUBLISHED BY WATERBROOK PRESS
2375 Telstar Drive, Suite 160
Colorado Springs, Colorado 80920
A division of Random House, Inc.

ISBN 1-57856-775-0

Copyright © 2005 by Dennis Jernigan
Interior images: property of Jupiter Images/Photos.com

Library of Congress Cataloging-in-Publication Data
Jernigan, Dennis.
    Giant killers : crushing strongholds, securing freedom in your life / Dennis Jernigan.—1st ed.
        p. cm.
    ISBN 1-57856-775-0
    1. Christian life. 2. Liberty—Religious aspects—Christianity. 3. Jernigan, Dennis. 4. Homosexuality—Religious aspects—Christianity. I. Title.
BV4509.5 .J48 2005
248.4—dc22   2004027052

Printed in the United States of America
2005—First Edition

10 9 8 7 6 5 4 3 2 1

To Melinda, Israel, Annē, Hannah, Glory,
Judah, Galen, Raina, Asa, and Ezra.
To those who have helped me slay the giants in my life.
To those who actively desire to slay the giants in their own lives.

CONTENTS

PART VIII: HEALING FOR THE INJURED

ACKNOWLEDGMENTS

Thanks to Eric Stanford who faithfully edited my words to sound like my heart.

To Bruce Nygren who helped guide me through the editorial process.

To Melinda—one of the best giant killers I know. Thanks for standing with me against so many giants.

To Steve Farrar—for the spiritual "attaboys."

To Mom and Dad, Peggy and Robert—for helping me lead others to confront the giants of life.

To Trish and Robin—for being armor bearers.

To Kathy Law—for making the journey so joyful.

To Tom P., Denny, Robert, Brian, Tim, and Tom H.—for being there for me.

To Kevin and Pam—for helping me enjoy life.

To Matt—for the shelter of your heart.

Preface

David, aiming his sling at the towering Goliath, set the pattern for every one of us. Oh, you and I don't face real giants who threaten our physical well-being. But then, giants don't always have to be physical.

- Are you overwhelmed by a craving for alcohol, drugs, or food?
- Does your desire for sexual fulfillment take you places you were never meant to go?
- Are you bogged down in depression and despair?
- Is fear or anxiety paralyzing you?
- Is anger, pride, or laziness spoiling your relationships?

If in honesty you would have to answer yes to one of these questions, or to a similar one, then you are facing a giant, and this book is for you.

- Are you aware of a spiritual problem in your life, and do you want to fix it, if you can?
- Do you feel as if you're getting nowhere in life—and hate that fact?
- Are you weary of the failures of your past dictating your present?
- Do you have visions and dreams and want to see them come to pass?
- Do you sense that the answer to your problem might lie outside yourself—in God?

If any of these questions resonate in your spirit, then you are ready for victory, and again, this book is for you.

If you will dare to read this book, I will challenge you to apply godly principles of freedom to your own giant, whatever it might be. Why? Because the strategy for defeating the giants in our lives is always the same: relationship with God Almighty through the redeeming power of Jesus Christ and the constant companionship of the Holy Spirit.

Does that sound thrilling to you? Or maybe a little like a letdown?

Today, it seems that most people want a quick fix—a fast-track how-to guide that will let them "get on with life." But if you're like me, you have grown skeptical of self-help guides that promise much and deliver little. While step-by-step instruction can be helpful, it can also be misleading. How many times have you gone through all the steps, only to find yourself just as entrenched in your problem as when you began the program?

Although this book will provide practical help along the way, it is primarily intended to draw you nearer to God in a devotional sense, for He must be the source of your victory. Approach the reading of this book, then, as a spiritual exercise. Don't rush through it, but instead consider each of its brief chapters as a morsel to be mentally savored.

To help you use this book for your spiritual good, each chapter ends with three spiritual exercises. The first, called "Truthstone," offers a set of related Scripture passages that you can read in your Bible and meditate upon. The second, "A Look Inside," provides a few questions that you can ask yourself to start applying the point of the chapter to your own life. The third, "Even in Their Sleep…" is based on Psalm 127:2, which says, "[God] gives to His beloved even in his sleep" (NASB). This section offers a thought or prayer idea that you can keep in your mind as you go to bed so that even as you are sleeping, God can be molding you into a giant killer.

By the grace of God, I have slain more than one giant in my life, and you will learn much of my story in this book. But the point you need to hear now is that on each occasion my spiritual healing has come about by virtue of my having an intimate relationship with

Jesus Christ. I want that same kind of healing for you! It will come through the same kind of relationship.

The only way God can help you is if you agree that God is God and you are not. Therefore, I suggest that before you read this book, you make the commitment to place your own agenda somewhere below God's. Lay down your own shaky conception of what is true, and stand upon the solid foundation of what your Creator calls truth, because as simple as it sounds, "You will know the truth, and the truth will set you free" (John 8:32).

Are you tired of the giants in your life winning all the battles? Would you like to slay some giants? You can. I say this not because that's what happened for me (though it has) but because I know God loves you and wants nothing but the best for you. Read on and begin now to trust God, allowing Him to replace the lies you have believed with His own glorious truth.

You have nothing to lose but bondage—and everything to gain of life and freedom!

PART

I

GIANTS IN
THE LAND

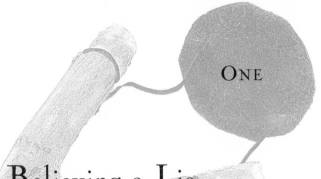

ONE

Believing a Lie

Y ou read about them in the pages of Scripture. You learn their stories in biographies of great Christians. And if you are like me, you have been privileged to know some of them personally. They are giant killers, men and women armed only (*only*—ha!) with faith in an almighty God and who have, in boldness, brought down the spiritual foes in their lives.

Some have felled sin, once looming tall and solid as Colossus. Some have quelled an anxiety that troubled their souls like a gale upon the water. Others have "done in" doubt, despair, or even the fear of death, our last enemy. What heroes, these! What heroines!

The stories of many of these giant killers will continue to be retold for generations to come, so thrilling are they. You may have your own stories of defeating the giants in your life, even if another behemoth stands before you now, and those stories mean so much to you. Every story of giant killing is valuable; every one inspiring, every one instructive.

Let me now tell you my own story of defeating a giant. My giant may be different from yours. Surely the way in which it grew in my life and the way in which God enabled me to defeat it are different from what you have experienced or will experience in giant killing. But I trust that as you hear my story, God will be at work in your heart, filling you with the confidence that you can overcome the giant challenging you now.

—

I was born in Sapulpa, Oklahoma. Soon after my birth, my parents moved to the farm my grandparents Samuel Washington Jernigan and Myrtle Mae Snyder had built—the farm where my father was raised. We lived three miles from the small town of Boynton, Oklahoma (population four hundred), where my brothers and I attended school.

The Lord gifted me from an early age to play the piano. By the time I was nine, I was playing for the worship times at First Baptist Church. This was also the church my grandfather Herman Everett Johnson had pastored. This was the church where my parents, Samuel Robert Jernigan and Peggy Yvonne Johnson, had met. My father had also "led singin'" there from the earliest I can remember (as he still does today).

When I was six or seven years old, my Grandmother Jernigan moved back to the farm, living in a trailer next to our farmhouse. Each day after school I could be found at my grandmother's house practicing piano (and conveniently forgetting about my chores). My grandma taught me how to play by ear and how to "chord" for "church playin'." She was always kind and supportive of me.

By contrast, over in the Jernigan household, we were not an affectionate family. While I did feel affection from my mother, I never remember receiving physical affection from my father or my brothers. In part, this was how families tended to act back then. And in part, the emotional distance was due to my daddy's working so hard. In addition to working the farm, he was employed by a utility company and worked as a mechanic for many years.

Since I have gotten older, God has reminded me of many ways my father expressed affection and love for me as I was growing up. My problem was not my father; my problem was that I believed a lie. Once Satan got his foot in the door of my heart, I perceived any rejection—no matter how big or small—as a lack of love from my dad (or whomever I thought was rejecting me at the time).

While from an early age I felt worthless, I discovered something: If I performed well, people would like me. So I tried to be the best in whatever I did, including schoolwork, basketball, and music. In the process I became a selfish person, usually at the expense of others.

It wasn't long, however, before I became frustrated, because no matter how well I performed, it never seemed to be good enough. What people thought was good—my outward performance—hid the deep hurts and failures of my heart. (And I must add that my daddy and mama never missed a single event I was involved in while growing up. This should have revealed a lot to me about their love.)

Now I need to tell you about the most painful part of my life, a part I long tried to hide. I allowed a sense of rejection to permeate every aspect of my life. (What I didn't realize was that Satan was lying to me, trying to keep me from God's plan for my life.) This included the sexual aspect of my life.

As a boy I needed a role model to show me the way to manhood. But because I felt rejected by the main man in my life, my father, I began to yearn for intimacy with other men in perverse ways. I remember having feelings of attraction toward the same gender from an early age. I hid this from others as best I could through my school and college years.

I attended Oklahoma Baptist University, and I look back on my four years there with fondness. Because of my lack of musical training while growing up, my musical studies at OBU were like learning a whole new language. But despite all the good that happened during those college years, that was also a time when I was secretly involved in homosexuality and was filled with confusion.

Being a young man in need of male affirmation, I was overwhelmed when an older man I respected began paying attention to me near the end of my time at college. As a "Christian," he said that he approached me from an attitude of caring about my well-being. To have someone like this call and ask how things were going for me made my life more bearable.

After many weeks of going out for a soda or simply riding around town and having him ask me how he could pray for me, I grew to trust this person immensely—so much so that I came to the point of asking him if I could share my deepest secret. I unloaded my burden about my sexual identity and immediately felt the weight lift from my shoulders. It felt wonderful!

The sense of lightness lasted only for moments. It came to an end when I realized this person was making a sexual advance toward me. And in those next few minutes, I felt utter despair as I gave up hope of ever getting help for my problem.

I came away from that encounter feeling so used and worthless that I decided to take my own life. I wanted peace more than I wanted to live. So I went home, turned on the gas stove, and lay down to die.

While thinking about how this outcome would be better for me as well as for my family and friends, my thoughts were interrupted by questions like *What is eternity really like?* and *Am I ready for what's out there?* I could not go on with the suicide. I got up from the floor, turned off the gas, and decided to live as I was obviously created to be—as a homosexual.

For the rest of the summer after my graduation, I traveled with a group promoting the university, and I lived in perverted relationship with another man. I thought I knew misery before, but this summer proved even more painful. I had given myself to what I perceived as my true identity and became more miserable than ever.

What was I going to do? Sometimes I thought I should go back to my plan of suicide. Other times, being a good Baptist boy, I decided that I should give God every opportunity to heal me. To me, that meant I should go to seminary. Yes, in my mind, it was either suicide or seminary!

But God had other plans.

—

Truthstone
Galatians 5:16-25
1 John 3:1-3

A Look Inside
1. What is the giant in my life?
2. Who provides a good role model for me as a giant killer? Why?
3. As I read the story of the growth of the giant in Dennis's life (even though his giant may be very different from mine), what does it suggest to me about the origins of my own giant?

"Even in Their Sleep…"
Tonight, spend some time thinking about your own life story as it has played out up to this point. As you do so, ask God to give you insights that will help you better understand—and heal from—whatever damage you may have in your life.

Two

Crying Out to God

Have you noticed that God has a habit of thinking that He is in charge? If it suits His purposes, He has no hesitation about stepping into our lives and sending us in a very different direction from what we have planned. I have experienced this behavior of His on more than one occasion, including when I was a young man.

Upon my graduation from Oklahoma Baptist University, I applied to seminary, assuming that since I had no direction for the next step in my life, I might as well pursue further education. I felt no peace about this decision, but I didn't know what else to do. Then three days before I was to leave for seminary, a former friend from OBU called and began to share some interesting ideas with me.

This friend had graduated a year before me. In the time between his graduation and mine, God had begun to impact his life greatly. As he sought God, he experienced deeper and deeper levels of intimacy with the Father. He told me of many of the things God had been doing in his life. I could tell from the passion in his voice that this was something different—or deeper—than I had ever known. He had my attention.

The conversation turned to the reason for my friend's call. God had been speaking to him—about me! He told me that God had come to him in a dream and had shown him many things He wanted to do in my life. In the dream, God was giving me many songs, and my friend and I and another alum from OBU were standing around a piano singing them.

I was moved by what my friend shared because his words had touched something deep within my heart: a longing to release the music I knew was in there. But he didn't stop there.

My friend went on to tell me that, in his dream, I was living with him and his mom. He further told me that he felt led to invite me to come and live with them. This in itself was overwhelming, but what he shared next awed me still more. He told me that his mother had been visited by the Lord with the *same dream* and that they both wanted to invite me to come and live with them and see what God would do.

This idea sounded just crazy enough to be God's will! Three days later, instead of starting at seminary, I was living in Del City, Oklahoma, beginning the fulfillment of a friend's dream and embarking upon a spiritual journey of my own.

In Del City my first priority was to find a job. Having my church music degree in hand, I quickly found a job—driving a school bus! That's right. The only job I could get was that of a school bus driver. (If you have ever worked toward a music degree or know someone who has, you will recognize God's sense of humor.)

In the mornings I had two bus routes with twenty-five minutes between them. During those twenty-five minutes, I would park my school bus in an abandoned housing subdivision and write in my journal. Journaling was the method I found most helpful in getting my most intimate thoughts out in the open before God. Day in and day out, I wrote of hurts, disillusionments, failures, emotions, and any other "soul data" that needed to come out. Later in the day I would go to the piano and write down my prayers, which for me happened to come out in the form of songs.

What I discovered in this process was that God really *was* concerned about my feelings, whatever they might be and however dark they might seem to me. I found the Father approachable and desiring *my* presence. In fact, I began to understand that God took more delight in my presence than I could possibly take in His.

After that first year of journaling, I felt God impress upon me that I should burn my writings. Page by page I burned my deepest heart cries and most horrendous secrets. Gently and tenderly the Father taught me that just as this picture of my past was being burned away, so too He had cleansed my past—and present and future—and had forgiven the wickedness of my heart.

In addition to the ways God was working in my life through my private times with Him, He began to move in other supernatural ways. I learned that a group called the 2nd Chapter of Acts was going to be in concert in Norman, Oklahoma, and somehow I knew that I was supposed to go.

As I listened to Annie Herring (one of the members of the group), I was overwhelmed by the love she spoke of. This was the love I had dreamed of but still couldn't believe was available to me. So I listened with great expectation—until she came to the song "Mansion Builder." This song caught my attention because of these simple lines:

Why should I worry?
Why should I fret?
I've got a Mansion Builder
Who ain't through with me yet!*

All of a sudden Annie stopped in the middle of the song and said, "There are those of you here who are dealing with things you have

---

*Annie Herring, "Mansion Builder," copyright © 1973 by Latter Rain Music. All rights controlled and administered by The Sparrow Corporation, PO Box 2120, Chatsworth, CA 91311. All rights reserved. International copyright secured. Used by permission.

never told anyone about. You are carrying those burdens, and that's wrong—that's sin, and you need to let those hurts go and give them to the Lord. We are going to sing the song again, and I want you to lift your hands to the Lord. And all of those burdens that you are carrying, I want you to place them in your hands and lift your hurts to Him."

This was all new to me—worship and praise. I had always thought before that this sort of thing was just an emotional response that didn't really mean anything. But do you know what it did for me? As I lifted my hands, God became more real to me than I had ever imagined. The lifting of my hands was more than a physical action; my hands were an extension of my heart.

I cried out, "Lord Jesus, I can't change me or the mess I've gotten myself into—but You can!" I acknowledged that I was totally helpless, and I turned everything in my life over to Jesus—my thoughts, my emotions, my body, my past. That night, November 7, 1981, I took responsibility for my own sins and yielded every right to Jesus, including my right to be loved and even my right to life.

At that point something wonderful began to take place in my life. I heard the Lord speak to my heart, "Dennis, I love you. Dennis, you are My child. Dennis, I will always love you."

It was then I lost the need to be accepted or loved by others in unhealthy ways, because I realized that Jesus would love me and accept me no matter what, even when I was rejected by others. It was also at this time that my perverse thoughts and desires were changed, and God began to replace them with holy thoughts about what sexual love is all about.

It was no coincidence that Satan attacked me at the point of my sexual drive. The sexual drive is a creative drive, and Satan knew that if he could pervert that drive in me, he could kill the creativity God had given me. He knew as well that if I were healed in my sexuality, I would spend the rest of my life praising my Father, his enemy.

Poor Satan. He lost on that one.

Truthstone
Psalm 34:12-19
Psalm 141:1-4

A Look Inside
1. How is God working in my life now to bring me near to Him?
2. When it comes to the giant in my life, how honest am I prepared to be with myself and with God?
3. Have I finally and completely given myself over to Jesus? If so, what was that like? If not, why not now?

"Even in Their Sleep..."
As you go to bed this evening, pour out your deepest feelings to God. Expect Him to dry your tears and to give you comfort as you sleep.

THREE

Helping Others Who Hurt

The songs began to flow, and I looked for others to sing them to and to sing them with. Two things quickly became apparent to me. First, I realized that my job was simply to seek God's heart. Second, I understood that the Good Shepherd never beats His sheep or forces them to worship Him. As I became more and more free in my expression to Him, others seemed to be drawn to Him *with* me.

Remember the dream my friend had? Just as in his dream, he and another friend (an alto) began to learn the songs with me in—you guessed it!—three-part harmony, much like the 2nd Chapter of Acts. Soon people were asking us to sing for meetings around Oklahoma City, then statewide and beyond. I sang with this trio for two years and can honestly say that those will always be some of my most precious memories.

But even as I was learning how to serve God with my gifts, I still had to face the truth of my past. Knowing I needed healing, God would not let me merely cover up my sin or try to forget about it. One stage in this healing occurred around this time—yet another divine setup.

A close friend found out about my former involvement in homosexuality and chose to speak to me about it. Instantly I knew I would be disgraced and rejected. When he confronted me, I ran from the house and continued to run until I could run no more.

Out of breath and out of hope, I cried out to God to speak to me.

At the same time, I looked into the evening sky, where I saw a puffy white cloud. This cloud looked like an old man with a beard and outstretched arms. Near this cloud was a smaller cloud in the shape of a lamb. As I watched, the bearded man engulfed the little lamb in his arms. I knew immediately that God was speaking to me, that this was what He wanted to do for me in this time of need. I returned to the house to face the music.

But that's not what happened. This friend was a true friend. He told me he loved me and was willing to stand with me as I walked through this time of deliverance in my life. And do you know what else happened? God began to bring others into my life who were willing to love me unconditionally and to walk with me through the trials of my life—no matter what—for my complete healing.

Foremost among those who came alongside me and loved me was Melinda Marie Hewitt, whom I married in 1983. Our marriage was the fulfillment of a dream for me. More than that, it was the beginning of the fulfillment of a promise God had given to me long before.

When I was about nine years old, I felt the Lord telling me that I would someday have a large family of my own—with nine children. By that age I was already identifying myself as homosexual. So I prayed, *Lord, You must be crazy. How can I have children if I have unnatural desires?* Yet the promise remained in my heart.

Today Melinda and I have nine wonderful children who fill our home and our hearts with joy.

When I married Melinda, I assumed that since I was healed, there was no need to share my past with her. But I soon realized that I was really still trying to hide, which meant that I still carried a burden and that I was still more concerned with what man thought of me than with what God thought of me.

As long as I hid these things from others, my relationships could never be what God wanted them to be, because in true love there is no fear. I was afraid to tell anyone because I thought no one would love me.

Why am I telling you this now? On July 18, 1988, I realized that God wanted to take the greatest failures and weaknesses of my life and make them my greatest strengths. I also realized that Satan wanted me to keep them hidden so he could use them against me. Not only this, but I knew that if I confessed my past freely, Satan would have no ammunition to use against me. So I shared what I have just told you with my church.

What do you think happened? Something beautiful. People who had been hurting just like me—and even more so—began to approach me. Men and women who were involved in homosexuality, women who were abused by their fathers, those who had been raped and had never told anyone, and those who had had abortions. As they confessed their sins and hurts, Jesus began healing their pasts.

On that day I publicly laid down my life and my reputation to serve Jesus in an awesome way. I want my life to be broken and poured out like the perfume the sinful woman used to wash Jesus's feet, even though others said she was foolish. Imagine this: The perfect King of the universe humbled Himself and gave up all His power and glory because He loves me. I can do no less.

Since the day I first shared my past publicly, God has called me to tell others what He has done for me—to lead others into intimacy with Jesus through music and worship. I hope that, in a way, this book will serve the same purpose. I am praying that this book will lead *you* closer to God.

Your circumstances, your sins, your wounds may all be different from mine, but the answer is still the same: Jesus. You may have been sinned against and wounded deeply. For those experiences, you are not guilty! Do not receive the false guilt that Satan would try to put on you because of circumstances that were beyond your control. I urge you instead to deal with your own heart and the things you were (and are) responsible for, such as attitudes, actions, thoughts, and feelings.

There is hope for the hurting. I've been there and found the way out, and I must share my story—the story of Jesus—with those who are hurting. Aren't we all hurting in one way or another?

The bottom line is this: I can't make it one day without the Lord. I ask Him to fill me with His Spirit day by day and moment by moment and to lead me. You see, we are all helpless and in need of a Father to care for us. And He is the Father who will never leave us or forsake us. He is the Father who enjoys our presence more than we could ever enjoy His.

Because of my relationship with Jesus, my healing will be a continual process until the day I die and see Him face to face.

Truthstone
Luke 7:36-50
John 10:1-18
2 Corinthians 1:3-7

A Look Inside
1. Am I hiding anything? If so, what harm might I be doing to myself by hiding?
2. What might God be doing right now to heal me, and how can I submit to Him?
3. When my giant is at last lying dead before me, how might I be able to help others who are facing similar giants?

"Even in Their Sleep…"
This evening, pray to the Father: *Lord, help me destroy the giant in my life, not for my sake, but for Your glory and for the good of others.*

FOUR

God's Strength in Our Weakness

R ight now I have a fear. It is that you, having read my story of slaying the giant of homosexuality, might be thinking something like this: *That's great for him. He evidently had something inside him that enabled him to be victorious over his problem. But me? I'm far too weak to fight the giant in my life. I've tried and failed, so I know.*

There's something you need to hear before we go any further: Your weakness is no obstacle to victory over your giant.

Because we want to appear strong and in control, we believe strength (that is, our *own* strength) is vital to our being giant killers. But this is not true. In fact, our wrong behavior is kept alive by just that sort of pride and self-reliance.

Of course, it *does* take strength to kill a giant, but God's Word is clear about where true strength lies: not in us but in God. The apostle Paul learned this lesson. Here is his story in his own words:

> To keep me from becoming conceited…there was given me a thorn in my flesh, a messenger of Satan, to torment me. Three times I pleaded with the Lord to take it away from me. But he said to me, "My grace is sufficient for you, for my power is made perfect in weakness." Therefore I will boast all the more gladly about my weaknesses, so that Christ's power

may rest on me. That is why, for Christ's sake, I delight
in weaknesses, in insults, in hardships, in persecutions,
in difficulties. For when I am weak, then I am strong.
(2 Corinthians 12:7-10)

"When I am weak, then I am strong"? Ridiculous!

Not ridiculous. If I try to make myself holy, I will fail. God, and
God alone, makes me who I am. I am the sheep; He is the Shepherd.
I am the clay; He is the Potter. I am the child; He is the Father. I am
the subject; He is the King. You get the idea.

When I am strong, I am worth as much as I do. But when I am
weak, I have worth because of who and whose I am—and there is rest
for my soul. When I am strong, I perform well to be accepted. I "do"
to "be." When I am weak, I perform well *because* I am accepted. I "do"
because I "am."

In 2 Chronicles we find the story of a king who shows us the
other side. He could legitimately say, "When I am strong, then I am
weak." King Uzziah was known for the strength of his army and for
his creative and massive weaponry.

Uzziah provided shields, spears, helmets, coats of armor, bows
and slingstones for the entire army. In Jerusalem he made
machines designed by skillful men for use on the towers and
on the corner defenses to shoot arrows and hurl large stones.
His fame spread far and wide, for he was greatly helped until
he became powerful.

But after Uzziah became powerful, his pride led to his
downfall. He was unfaithful to the LORD his God. (26:14-16)

Did you catch that? "He was greatly helped [by the Lord] until
he became powerful"! The Lord withdrew His aid when Uzziah be-

came prideful, and so it was revealed just how weak Uzziah really was in his own strength. Uzziah fell from power and died in misery rather than the glory that could have been his.

When we operate in our own strength and that strength is guarded by our pride, we have only one place to go, and that is down. So how does one become strong in weakness?

Paul did it this way: He changed his vantage point. He changed the way he approached his thorn—his giant. He approached it from God's perspective, realizing that this thorn was not the identifying mark of his life. This thorn, in essence, became another opportunity for Paul to draw near to God. Paul changed his approach so drastically that he stopped whining about his predicament and began doing something outrageous. He began to *boast* in his weakness!

By boasting in his weakness, Paul was really glorifying God's strength. Whatever the apostle accomplished was obviously the work of God. Paul's strange boasting really put him in his proper place and God in His.

For me, boasting in my weakness meant choosing to see my past through the filter of God's redemptive work by the blood of Jesus Christ. I had been forgiven, so I needed to think, feel, and act as a forgiven one. Life became like driving a car. I wouldn't get very far by focusing on the rearview mirror. That mirror is there to help me maintain the integrity of the journey.

I remember my affliction and my wandering,
  the bitterness and the gall.
I well remember them,
  and my soul is downcast within me.

Yet this I call to mind
  and therefore I have hope:

Because of the LORD's great love we are not consumed,
    for his compassions never fail.
They are new every morning;
    great is your faithfulness. (Lamentations 3:19-23)

I take my complaints before God, but then I drive my car not by looking constantly in the rearview mirror but by focusing on the goal of my journey. That goal: to know Jesus Christ and to enjoy being known by Him.

I tried for years to overcome homosexuality and feelings of rejection in my own strength. Freedom did not come for me until that November evening in 1981 when I finally realized the truth that I could not save myself. On that night I gave up and said, *Lord Jesus, I can't change me or the mess I've gotten myself into—but You can!* And when I made that act of confession, my heart broke and I became weak.

Brokenness can come in a couple of ways. Circumstantial brokenness—events of life that cause us to see how weak and needy we really are—can be used by God to bring us to deep and abiding trust in Him. Internal brokenness—a breakdown of wrong belief systems—can be used by God to completely transform a mind and bring emotional stability.

I have known both kinds of brokenness—and so have you.

Who would have thought that God would take what I consider my greatest failure and use it to bring Himself the greatest glory? Certainly not me! But that has been the case. And that's why I now boast in my weakness so God's power may be manifested in me.

Do we *have* to boast in our weaknesses? No. As my friend Jack Taylor says, "You can be miserable if you want to."

I can be weak. In fact, I have a near-perfect record in that area. But that is just what I have to boast about.

We boast in weakness so God can be our strength. We boast in the insults of life so He can affirm us in eternity. We boast in the distresses of life so He can show forth His peace and love through the stormy gales of existence. We boast in persecutions so He can pour out upon us His abundant grace. We boast in every difficulty so He can show forth His mighty power and redeeming love to those who do not know there is hope or a way out.

Now, go boast in your weakness and see the power of almighty God take you to levels of freedom and intimacy you never imagined in this life. Praise the Lord!

Truthstone
Isaiah 41:10
Zechariah 4:6
2 Corinthians 12:1-10

A Look Inside
1. Whose strength—mine or God's—have I been relying on to defeat my giant?
2. How could looking at myself as weak actually help me?
3. What will it take for me to be ready to boast in my weakness?

"Even in Their Sleep…"
Spend time confessing your weakness to God and throwing yourself utterly upon His resources for victory over your giant.

I Can't Live Without You

I have lived so many lies
So many things I'd love to erase
So many storms I would not have survived
Except for Your redeeming grace
I have known both plenty and lack
I've known both joy and deepest despair
And ev'rytime I have ever looked back
In joy and sorrow You have been there

Life without You is not life
At best, it's simply futility
Deciding what is right in my own eyes
I wind up failing so miserably
So many times, Lord, I've doubted You
You never stop believing in me
I want my life to be lived in such a way
The whole world all around me can see that…

I can't live without You here in my life
I can't live without You. How could I survive?
I know life without You is just getting by
I can't live without You in my life

PART

II

FIVE GIANTS,
FIVE STONES

FIVE

Why Five Stones?

A boy kneels by a swiftly running stream and selects five stones worn smooth by the tumbling of the water. The boy slips the stones into his bag, grips the sling he knows how to aim with deadly accuracy, and rises to face a foe who towers over him like a pillar of rock. As it turns out, minutes later the boy will need only one of his carefully chosen stones to topple the giant.

We all know that scene from the story of David and Goliath, and we all are impressed by a teenager whose faith in God was so great that he could approach an enemy who had frightened grown men. But have you ever wondered, *Why* five *stones?* Until a few years ago, I wondered about it. Why would God lead David to choose five stones when he would need only one? I stopped wondering when I heard a speaker talk about Goliath's four brothers.

The speaker was taking a minor liberty in referring to these other giants as Goliath's "brothers," since probably only one of them was literally the brother of the giant whom David slew. But it *is* an often-overlooked fact that the Bible describes not the slaying of just one giant but the slaying of five (see 1 Samuel 17; 2 Samuel 21:15-22; 1 Chronicles 20:4-7).

Three of these other giants were called Ishbi-Benob, Saph (or Sippai), and Lahmi, while the fourth goes unnamed in the pages of Scripture. Lahmi is the one described as "the brother of Goliath" (1 Chronicles 20:5). The others are identified as "descendants of

Rapha" (verse 8). It is possible, Bible scholars tell us, that Rapha is not a name at all but instead means "the giant." Were these men, then, sons or grandsons of Goliath? On the other hand, the word *Rapha* could indicate that all of these giants were descended from the race of Rephaites, giants who lived in Canaan generations earlier (see Deuteronomy 2:20-21; 3:11,13).

Regardless of the exact identity of this fearsome foursome, the Bible does tell us this: David himself did not kill them. Rather, other men who were followers and admirers of David killed them in the spirit of David's triumph over Goliath. (See 1 Chronicles 20:4-7.) Symbolically, it was as if David had distributed his remaining four stones to these men so they could reproduce his signature victory for the glory of God.

This raises another question. After David killed Goliath and went on to become king of Israel, did he think that the threat of giants was behind him, or did he know that more giants were out there waiting to be conquered? Did he have any inkling that his forces would have to face the likes of Lahmi, Saph, and the rest?

I believe David had every reason to suspect that once he had defeated Goliath, other giants would not be far behind. There must have been rumors that Goliath was not a lone figure but a member of a family in which possessing great size and equivalent strength was the norm. Others like Goliath would be coming to avenge his defeat if they could. It would be a case of one giant after another.

My friend, I ask you, how much like dealing with sin is that? We defeat one sin or deal with one deficiency in our lives, and as soon as we are content that the issue is settled, we realize that we have uncovered a whole nest of the varmints!

A little freedom in Christ leads to more freedom. And so hatred rises in the black heart of our Enemy, Satan, because he despises the freedom being birthed in our lives. It stirs him to try to retain his grip on our lives by any means he can. He raises up obstacle after obstacle in an attempt to keep us from advancing in the power of God. If he can trip us up or cause us to give up in the fight, then he has served his purpose as destroyer of all that is holy about us and our identity.

When I made my decisive turn away from homosexuality in 1981, I felt light and free because that particular Goliath lay dead at my feet. What a relief! I thought I could rest at last. But then I heard a familiar roar in the distance. Could it be? Oh yes, it could. And as another giant came into view, I understood.

There is never just one giant. There are many, and it is my job to defeat all of the giants in my life. These are other temptations, other flaws in my makeup, other attacks on my self-image or my position as a child of God. Somehow I know that each one will try to revive the legacy of sin and shame that my original Goliath brought to me.

Once I asked Christ, the ultimate Giant Killer, "Why do the giants keep coming? When will I get to rest from the battles?"

And the Giant Killer spoke. "The giants keep coming because that is what giants do. Sin gives birth to many giants. Sin always begets more sin unless it is cut off. I cut it off at the Cross, but it is up to you to put that victory into practice in your own life.

"You, giant killer, must crucify your flesh. Crucifixion is not an instant death; it can be long and excruciating. The flesh does not want to die. But once you have begun the process, it will be completed. So do not focus on where you are in that process, but instead focus on where that process will leave you.

"When will you rest? Even in the heat of battle. I tell you, rest does not always look like a hammock stretched between two trees on a lazy summer evening. Rest can mean looking to Me and My grace even as you swing your weapon. Rest is simply being with Me.

"I promise you this: I will be with you every step of the way. I will hold you together when you feel that you could fall apart. And I will be there to celebrate with you when at last your battles are at an end."

Even as the peace and assurance of those words flooded my soul,

I heard the roar of yet another giant. But instead of letting it bring weariness to me, I saw it as an opportunity to experience God's grace in a greater way. I am not a pitiful, struggling sinner. I am a giant killer!

Come with me as I lead you through some discoveries about freedom that I have found by thinking about the battles against the five giants in Scripture. And see if you can identify with the circumstances faced by David and his mighty men. We will look at the names of the giants and see how they illustrate the way certain giants operate and how we might defeat them.

Giant after giant? Bring them on!

Truthstone
Isaiah 40:29-31
Romans 6:5-14
Colossians 3:5-10

A Look Inside
1. When have I been surprised by an additional giant appearing on the horizon after I had already defeated one?
2. Do I have the commitment to keep on fighting my whole life through?
3. Am I able to find my rest in Jesus even in the midst of battle?

"Even in Their Sleep..."
Seek God for a renewal of courage and strength. Ask Him for the determination not just to wait for giants to come to you but to seek them out!

Six

Goliath: Giant of Shame

Picture Goliath in your mind. He stood over nine feet tall, a foot taller than the usual home-ceiling height today. (If Goliath were alive in our day, his height wouldn't be enough to get him into *Guinness World Records*, but it would certainly mean that NBA scouts would be swarming all around him.) He was covered from head to legs in bronze armor that weighed well over a hundred pounds. That fact, combined with the fact that his spear shaft was huge, with an iron tip weighing fifteen pounds, goes to show that Goliath had the muscles to match his size. Would you want to face this guy?

Next, picture David as he was at that time. He was presumably a slim, young teenager of average height, since we know he was too small to wear the armor of King Saul (a tall man). David was probably wiry for his age, due to his active outdoor life as a shepherd, and so he could whip a rock out of a sling powerfully enough to sink it into the forehead of one overgrown, overconfident Philistine. But, of course, David was no bodybuilder. If he had stood close to Goliath, he would easily have been swallowed up in the giant's shadow.

And it was this ruddy-faced lad who ran up to the giant, whirled a sling around to build up speed, and then let go. Amazing!

But you know all this. If you attended Sunday school as a child, you certainly heard the story. You've read it in your Bible during your personal devotional time. Maybe you read a version of it (probably over and over again) to your children from a Bible storybook. But I'll tell you something about this story that I bet you don't know.

What do you think the name *Goliath* means? If you think it means "giant," you're as mistaken as I was for a long time. Goliath actually means "to be disgracefully stripped naked."

How fitting. Goliath's power over the men of Israel was not one of physical power, strong as he was, but rather one of intimidation. Twice a day for forty days, the champion of Philistia came forward and presented himself for any Israelite soldier who wanted to take him on. When he shouted his defiance, though, they all ran from him in fear. Long before the forty days were up, those men must have been feeling thoroughly ashamed of themselves. They had been stripped naked of their pretensions to courage.

We can sympathize, can't we? How often does our own sin or weakness leave us feeling naked, emotionally or spiritually? We feel exposed before God and potentially exposed before others, if our sin should leak out for everyone to see. We feel ashamed that someone might see our fallen state. We try to hide what is wrong with us, but down deep we know it is no good. The sin or failing is still there, ever threatening to be seen.

Our emotional or spiritual nakedness then makes us more vulnerable to whatever caused it in the first place. The giant in our lives fills us with hopelessness and despair. We believe that we can never defeat it. And so we reason that we may as well give in, even make friends with the Enemy. Rather than turn to God for mercy and forgiveness, we fall victim to the subtle temptation of the Enemy due to our guilt and shame, and we fall again. Now we are caught in a cycle that becomes more difficult to break out of with each passing day.

The question for us is this: Will we be like David and take up a stone against the giant, or will we be like the Israelite soldiers and run in fear?

God has given us a stone perfectly formed to strike down the

Goliath giant of shame. It is the stone of our identity in Christ. Satan, the Accuser, reminds us of all the wrong we've done, all the weakness we embody, and all the shame we have earned. But Christ, our Advocate, says, "There is now no condemnation for this one. He is a child of God, forgiven and redeemed and one day to be glorified."

When I was struggling with homosexuality, I felt hopeless. I believed that this giant that taunted me mercilessly would never be defeated in my life. And that's why I was overjoyed on the day when the Lord revealed that He had already paid the debt for my sin and that I had been given a brand-new identity. I am who God says I am, not who my Enemy says I am. I need no longer be ashamed.

The other side of the coin flipped over when I realized that God had done the work of redemption and that it was now up to me to do the work of learning how to be His son—of learning how to be a giant killer. He released me from my guilt and shame, but it was up to me to take up the stones that would be required to defeat the giants in my life and then trust Him for the grace to face them honestly and boldly, regardless of how those giants lied to me or taunted me.

Living contrary to my past feelings and former ways of identifying myself was not easy at first. What kept me on that journey toward freedom was knowing that God loved me and even liked being with me. How did I know that?

When I began having my own children, I discovered that I would do anything to see them happy and successful. I discovered that I not only loved them but liked them as well. I liked being with them. My great revelation? If I, as an earthly father, can say and feel and practice such things, how much more will my heavenly Father do so toward me?

Putting on that truth—the truth of who God says I am—has helped me defeat the giants of shame and fear that once held me so captive that I did not want anyone else to even know what I had been delivered from. My, how things have changed! Now God uses my greatest failure to bring Him glory and to draw others who are trapped in the strongholds of various giants into the freedom that is found only in Him.

Truthstone
Genesis 2:25; 3:6-7
1 Samuel 17
Psalm 139:1-12

A Look Inside
1. How has the giant in my life made me feel stripped naked, spiritually or emotionally?
2. How have I responded to that feeling of disgraceful exposure?
3. Am I now focused more on my identity as God's child than I am on my past shame?

"Even in Their Sleep…"
Before bed, invite the Holy Spirit to show you what it looks like to live in the full consciousness that your shame has been erased through Christ.

SEVEN

Ishbi-Benob: Giant of Discouragement

Y ou thought I was kidding about those other giants? Read this:

Once again there was a battle between the Philistines and
Israel. David went down with his men to fight against the
Philistines, and he became exhausted. And Ishbi-Benob, one
of the descendants of Rapha, whose bronze spearhead weighed
three hundred shekels and who was armed with a new sword,
said he would kill David. But Abishai son of Zeruiah came to
David's rescue; he struck the Philistine down and killed him.
(2 Samuel 21:15-17)

This encounter occurred many years after David's boyhood show-
down with Goliath. Those intervening years had brought tremendous
change for David. He had become king, raised a family, beat down
rebellion, and waged many wars. The years had given him much, but
they had also taken away some of his physical strength. In battle with
the Philistines one day, David became exhausted and vulnerable to
the enemy's secret weapon: a giant named Ishbi-Benob.

Fortunately, David had more resources this time around. He had
gathered a group of extraordinary soldiers around him, an inner circle

of guards known as "David's mighty men." (What a cool name!) Among these were a group known as the Thirty and an even more elite group known as the Three. These mighty men were responsible for many legendary deeds, including the time a trio of them broke through enemy lines just to fulfill a desire for water that David had casually expressed (see 2 Samuel 23:8-39).

Perhaps the greatest of all these mighty men was David's nephew Abishai, the chief of the Three. When Ishbi-Benob was advancing with his heavy-duty spear and the new sword he was no doubt proud of, and a weakened David was facing real peril, Abishai stepped in and struck down the Philistine. So much for giant number two.

But let's rewind the tape just a bit to the point where Ishbi-Benob is vowing to kill David and is hacking down Israelite soldiers to get at the exhausted king. What do you think the Israelites were thinking at that time? What do you think David himself was thinking? I imagine that every Israelite on the field of battle, with the exception of Abishai, was thinking, *Oh no! Not again!*

A Philistine giant had stymied an army of Israel before, and now here was another one. When was there ever going to be an end to such foes? What good was further fighting going to do?

Do you hear the voice of discouragement? Do you recognize its sound as it echoes inside your own head?

The name Ishbi-Benob comes from a root word meaning "to retreat," and retreat is just what this giant made the Israelites want to do. We, too, want to retreat when attacks are renewed upon us. How often do we allow the giants in our lives to cause us to fall away in dread—to want to give up—because we "just knew this was going to happen again"? How sad!

Let me assure you of this: Just because we have to face a giant does not mean that giant determines our destiny or our identity. Just because we are tempted in a certain way does not mean we have failed. Jesus was tempted in every manner as we are, yet He was without sin (see Hebrews 4:15). So when we say, "No one understands" or "I am constantly tempted, so this just must be the way I am," we are not viewing ourselves or our sin realistically.

What, then, is the "Abishai" that will defeat the Ishbi-Benob giant of discouragement for us? Or, to put it another way, what is the stone that will slay this giant? It is having a divine perspective on our situation.

From where we stand, all we see is a giant bearing down upon us. No wonder we feel hopeless. No wonder we despair. But we cannot see everything. God's truth is greater than all the Enemy's lies. If we will look at our situation from the higher perspective of heaven, we will renew our hope. And as we will hold on and refuse to quit, we will see what God will do in our lives.

I have been made miserable and been driven to the point of despair many times in my quest to live a life that honors God. I have been tempted to believe that life and its many battles are hopeless. I have been disillusioned and have felt like giving up from the sheer constancy of the bombardment. But I have learned to "resist the devil" (James 4:7), not retreat.

Why have I become more hopeful, more determined to carry on? Because I have realized something: The blows the Enemy inflicts upon me never amount to more than a surface wound. They can never penetrate the seal that guards my heart. God still loves me and cares for me, and He is going to step in and rescue me as long as I am trusting in Him.

Whatever your giant may be—anxiety, fear, sin, whatever—it is not the overwhelming opposition that it appears to be. Take your focus off the giant and put it on the power of God inside you through His Spirit. Put it on the truths of Scripture that overturn every false-hood. Put it on the resources God offers through His church and on the certainty that He will rescue and preserve you through all that may come.

The view from heaven looks pretty good. Change your perspective. Renew your hope.

———

Truthstone
2 Samuel 21:15-17
Isaiah 35:3-4

A Look Inside
1. What do I tend to be discouraged about as I fight the giants in my life?
2. What false words of hopelessness have I heard echoing inside my head?
3. Right now, what am I most discouraged about? If I were to sit down and talk to God about this, what might He say to give me hope?

"Even in Their Sleep…"
Ask God to place you, figuratively speaking, on a high cliff overlooking your life so that you can view your past, present, and future as He does.

EIGHT

Saph: Giant of Fear

The name of this giant sounds like a type of infection! I am sure David and his mighty men must have been getting tired of giants, as one tires of a sickness that keeps recurring. In 2 Samuel 21:18 we are told that "in the course of time, there was another battle with the Philistines, at Gob. At that time Sibbecai the Hushathite killed Saph, one of the descendants of Rapha."

How often do we enjoy victory in our spiritual lives one day and then come face to face with an attack in that very same area the very next day? I believe this is a common pattern, and like David and his men, we should be prepared for such attacks. How do we prepare?

First, let us look at what the name *Saph* means: "to snatch away" or "to wait at the threshold." Saph may have been one of those soldiers sent out on reconnaissance by the Philistine leadership. Perhaps he lurked in the known hangouts of King David, waiting at the threshold for just the right moment to lunge in and pluck David's life away.

Is our battle with habitual sin or other problems in our lives going to be any different? Is it not reasonable for us to expect that our failings will seek to leap out at us at a vulnerable moment and attempt to draw us back into the ungodly patterns we want to leave? To think otherwise would be foolishness!

Far back in human history, the Lord said to Cain, eldest son of Adam and Eve, "If you do not do what is right, sin is crouching at your door; it desires to have you, but you must master it" (Genesis 4:7). And just so, sin is crouching at the door for each of us. If we don't master it, it will master us.

Have you ever gone to one of those scary movies in which, at the moment when you're least expecting it, someone or something terrifying suddenly lunges out at the hero? The hero leaps back—and simultaneously, right there in your theater seat, you set the record for the sitting high jump! The fear of what evil may lurk in darkness and in hiding places runs deep in the human psyche.

Your battle against the giant in your life will subject you to fear. A woman I know was struggling with anxiety, and one of her deepest fears was that her condition would get worse and she would lose her mind. Someone else was struggling with overeating, and he feared that he would lose all control over his eating and literally eat himself to death.

I bet you could name your own fears without a moment's hesitation.

Let's be honest here: Giant killing is no easy task. It always brings fear. Indeed, any realistic story of a hero going into battle takes into account the fears that arise in his heart. But the story will also tell how the hero overcame his fears on the way to conquering his enemy.

There is no need for you to give in to your fear. God has provided the stone that will fell this giant. It is the stone of intimacy with God, and we get a glimpse of this stone in the story of the defeat of Saph.

Who defeated Saph? Just as in the destruction of Ishbi-Benob, it was one of David's devoted men—in this case, Sibbecai. I find it interesting that the name *Sibbecai* means "to wrap around as trees surround and enclose a protected pasture."

When I drive around the countryside surrounding my own farm, I am always intrigued when I see a stand of trees that have been planted in orderly fashion. Because of my background as a farm boy, I know that many of these stands of trees were planted over a hundred years ago to serve as a shield for livestock, protecting them from Oklahoma's

harsh winter winds. Though many no longer serve their original purpose, these trees still stand as a testament to their lasting power.

How much like Sibbecai is God? He is always surrounding us
with His presence. The fact that we do not always rely upon that presence but, rather, run away from it to embrace the very enemies we
need to run *from,* is not God's fault. We wonder why we keep falling
into the same old failures, but we never take responsibility for seeking
God and His protection from the onslaught of those sly and schem-
ing giants we *know* we are going to be facing!

Are you willing to rely upon the Lord's protection whenever you
are faced with the fears that come with giant killing? You can have
that protection as you draw close to God, seeking greater intimacy
with Him.

I have noticed that when my children were small, if they became
frightened by something—perhaps a thunderstorm outside or a bad
dream that had awakened them—all they had to do was snuggle
against me to feel comforted. We can snuggle up against God when
we are scared too. He is our *Abba*—our "Papa"—and He loves nothing better than for us to get close to Him.

The book of James gives us a short course in how to defeat Satan.
It says that in relation to Satan, we are to be like the kind of magnet
that repels another magnet. "Resist the devil, and he will flee from
you" (James 4:7). More to our point here, James says that in relation
to God, we are to be like the kind of magnet that attracts Him.
"Come near to God and he will come near to you" (verse 8). The
Lord is always there, right next to us, waiting for us to draw near to
Him so that He can respond in just the same way.

Oh, I beg you, my friend, draw near to the Lover of your soul.
He so wants you to know Him as intimately as He already knows you.
Hear His voice calling out to you, "Come, My child. Come close to
Me. Feel My comfort wrap around you like a hug. I will protect you.

I will preserve you through every danger. With Me, you need fear no more but only delight in My presence, where you have always been meant to be."

Truthstone
2 Samuel 21:18; 1 Chronicles 20:4
Philippians 3:8-11
James 4:7-8

A Look Inside
1. What do I fear most about the giant I am fighting?
2. Is God more like a mere acquaintance to me, or is he my dearest friend?
3. In what way(s) do I most need to draw near to God in intimacy?

"Even in Their Sleep…"
Ask God to come to you tonight and give you a sense of just how passionately He wants to be known and sought by you.

NINE

Lahmi: Giant of Evil Desires

I told you that giants just keep coming. "In another battle with the Philistines, Elhanan son of Jair killed Lahmi the brother of Goliath the Gittite, who had a spear with a shaft like a weaver's rod" (1 Chronicles 20:5). This giant carried a weapon just as oversized as that possessed by his more famous brother (see 1 Samuel 17:7), but he, too, succumbed to the skill of one of David's great warriors.

The name *Lahmi* means "foodful." It speaks of our ungodly cravings not just for food but also for selfish power, excessive wealth, or whatever other kind of sinful indulgence we might desire. The Lahmi in my life was lust, a misdirected and unacceptable sexual desire. Your Lahmi may be different from mine, but most likely you will have no trouble identifying whatever "foodfulness" your own sinful nature desires.

But what lies beneath all of these evil desires? I think I have discovered what it is.

I'm struck by the way I pronounce this giant's name: Lah-*me*. It's an appropriate pronunciation, for I have observed that in fighting the giants in our lives, we tend to focus so intensely upon ourselves and our circumstances that we take on the "It's all about me" attitude. When all we see, feel, and do is focused upon us, then we become self-centered and prideful, and our evil desires easily take over. The devil knows that if he can draw our attention away from God and focus it upon ourselves, the battle for our souls will be a walk in the park for him.

God's Word says this about evil desires and pride: "Everything in the world—the cravings of sinful man, the lust of his eyes and the boasting of what he has and does—comes not from the Father but from the world" (1 John 2:16). Such human-centered thinking is not from God. To think in this manner requires that we place ourselves upon the throne that rightly belongs to God. As long as God is not on the throne of our hearts, we will never overcome any of the giants in our lives, whether those giants involve illicit sex, overeating, drunkenness, or some other stronghold.

I speak with men and women all the time who have given up on God because they have "given up to God so many times" but have never been changed. There's that self-centered attitude again. "I want to be changed—I want it now and I want it on my own terms!"

Pride is a killer. Pride keeps us from real life because it can be sustained only by deception and dishonesty. How different things would be if a person would humble his or her heart and ask God for healing—and then *obey* His leading!

Here's what God says about humbling oneself:

All of you, clothe yourselves with humility toward one
another, because,

"God opposes the proud
     but gives grace to the humble."

Humble yourselves, therefore, under God's mighty hand, that
he may lift you up in due time. (1 Peter 5:5-6)

The prerequisite for being lifted up is kneeling down.

Perhaps you have said something like this in the past:

- "No one understands me and my problems."
- "Everyone is against me. People want to keep me from being who I am."
- "I asked God to heal me, but nothing ever happened."
- "My feelings are so intense that you just wouldn't understand."

Sounds like a toddler who isn't getting her way, doesn't it?

Perhaps we need to grow up and take responsibility for our own choices, for our own feelings, for our own actions and thought life. We need to crucify our flesh—our self-centered desires—and instead of expecting God to do all the work, develop a relationship with Him and then *do what He says!*

How can a toddler learn to run if she expects someone else to carry her? How can we overcome the giants in our lives if we think we deserve immediate gratification?

If we really want to defeat the giants in our lives, we must first humble ourselves—step down from the throne and enthrone God in His rightful place as Lord and King of our feelings, Lord and King of our desires, Lord and King of all we are. Only when He is on the throne where He deserves to be are we truly changed.

When we acknowledge Jesus Christ as Savior and believe that God has raised Him from the dead, we are saved. That salvation also means we gain a new identity, regardless of our past failures or sinful cravings. Second Corinthians 5:17 says, "If anyone is in Christ, he is a new creation; the old has gone, the new has come!" Galatians 6:15 tells us that "what counts is a new creation." When we have become new creations, one of the greatest gifts of God is His grace in our lives. Grace, simply put, is the power of God to overcome anything.

Once we have humbled ourselves and received His grace, we can even learn to lust and crave in a righteous and holy manner. How is that? Let me explain.

When we become new creations, our core identity is forever changed. We also attain the power through God to endure all manner of Enemy tactics against our souls. (Yeah, I know. The devil keeps on attacking. But that's okay—you'll see.) Becoming someone brand new inside is like becoming a little baby in the hands of the Father. We must trust Him to nurture us and rebuild us as He tears away the old identity and replaces it with the new.

That change is vividly portrayed in the account of Lazarus being raised from the dead (see John 11:1-44). Jesus called Lazarus forth from the dead, just as He has called us forth from the death of our old lives. Lazarus was still wrapped in the clothes of death, just as we carry many of the wrappings from our old lives. But Jesus commanded those around Lazarus to loosen the grave clothes, and He calls us to do the same with our old lives.

When we continually refer to ourselves based upon the old grave clothes, we see only death and despair, and we want to give up. In that wrapped-up state, we find it difficult to walk in our new lives because of all the old constraints. But Jesus wants us to be free of the old ways of thinking. He desires that we not only walk in freedom but run and fight and rejoice in that freedom as well.

Instead of lusting after the old, we must learn to put it off and put on the new. With this new freedom, we can crave knowing God better and respecting Him for who He is. If He is Lord and King (and He surely is!), then we should be worshiping him. The stone that kills the giant of evil desires, along with the self-centeredness that underlies it, is the stone of praise and worship. When we worship, God is put in His proper place, and we are put in ours. Our selfish sin has to die.

Are you willing to humble yourself and step down from the throne of your life? Are you willing to crown Jesus Christ as King of your heart and life? Would you like to learn how to be a giant killer, a grace receiver, an intimate knower of the God of the universe? Then I have one piece of advice for you: Worship Him.

Truthstone
2 Samuel 21:19; 1 Chronicles 20:5
Romans 8:5-11
Psalm 147

A Look Inside
1. What is the Lahmi (wicked craving) in my life?
2. In what way is a prideful or self-centered attitude expressed through the giant in my life?
3. What role do praise and worship play in my life?

"Even in Their Sleep..."
Before going to bed tonight, ask God to fill you with a better sense of His love and majesty so that you will be moved to worship Him.

TEN

"Six Fingers": Giant of Enslavement to Sin

The fifth and last giant, unlike his kinsmen Goliath, Ishbi-Benob, Saph, and Lahmi, is given no name in the Bible. Instead, he is identified by an unusual physical characteristic that today is known as polydactyly: Rather than having five fingers or five toes, he had six. This trait must have made him seem more extraordinary and more fearsome to others of his day than even his great height did.

Let's call this giant "Six Fingers." Here is the story of his end and the end of his story (following the now-familiar pattern):

> In still another battle, which took place at Gath, there was a huge man with six fingers on each hand and six toes on each foot—twenty-four in all. He also was descended from Rapha. When he taunted Israel, Jonathan son of Shimeah, David's brother, killed him. (2 Samuel 21:20-21)

As I have meditated on this story, I have begun to wonder if perhaps God chose not to include this giant's name in His Book because He wanted us to focus on the giant's unusual physical attribute instead. With six fingers on each hand, this giant (you would think) would have a great advantage: Anything or anyone he wanted to get a hold on would be held in a seemingly unshakable grasp. Imagine being an Israelite soldier unlucky enough to fall into the clutches of this huge Philistine. Imagine all those fingers closing around your neck and *squeezing*. Imagine being lifted up, up, up...

It can be the same with the personal giants we fight. Perhaps you feel that the problem in your life—let's say it's a drinking problem—has such a tight grip on you that you can never wriggle free. You tell yourself that you have changed. You go to group support meetings; you drive the long way home from work to avoid your favorite bar. You try everything you can think of, in short, to keep yourself from liquor. But it seems that sooner or later, alcohol always calls to you and you cannot help answering.

Six Fingers has got his hold on you. He's taunting you just like that Philistine giant Goliath taunted the armies of Israel. Six Fingers is saying to you, "You'll never get out of this. You're stuck, trapped—face it! This is your destiny. Your future will be just like your present, if not worse. Don't even think it could be different." He's saying that you're forever enslaved to sin.

In my own life, the sin of homosexuality seemed to have an unshakable grasp on me. I eventually became convinced that its grip was so strong and such a part of my life that I could not live without it. As a little boy I used to beg God to change me. But nothing ever happened, and I honestly felt that the grip of this giant in my life was beyond my capacity to break. And indeed it was. I needed someone to break this power for me.

In the Bible story it was David's nephew Jonathan who rescued David and the rest of the Israelite forces from the threat posed by Six Fingers. Instead of being cowed by the giant, Jonathan proved that he was up to the task of silencing this mocking behemoth. Jonathan proved that this giant's grip was not so unshakable as it had seemed.

My "Jonathan" was Jesus Christ. In fact, He is the only "Jonathan" any of us will see defeat our personal giants. We are not able to break the grip of sin in our lives on our own—we are too weak and sinful. And however helpful preachers, counselors, and loving friends or family members may be, they are not capable of breaking that grip for us either. Only Christ has the power to accomplish the heroic task of emancipating us.

David's nephew Jonathan found a way of slipping out of the clutches of Six Fingers. With Christ's help, we can slip out of temptation's clutches just as surely. First Corinthians 10:13 tells us, "No temptation has seized you except what is common to man. And God is faithful; he will not let you be tempted beyond what you can bear. But when you are tempted, he will also provide a way out so that you can stand up under it."

Your temptation is common to man. You are not special—but God is faithful! With every temptation, He will be waiting with an escape plan. I know that sounds incredible, but if God is God, then we should be able to find those escape routes because He never leaves us or forsakes us. His gift to us is His presence in times of temptation, when the grip of sin seems unshakable.

With God in your life, you can do more than slip out of the grip of your particular sin or problem; you can also move completely beyond it. You can head into a future that is far more wonderful than the present you are now living. You can have a life that's spiritually and emotionally healthy and brings joy both to God and to you. You can if you believe in God and believe in yourself as you are changed by Him. The stone that's effective against the giant of sin, then, is the stone of dreams for the future.

I urge you to take up this stone by faith and ask God to fill your mind with images of a different future for yourself. He has a track record of giving His devoted followers amazing visions and dreams.

Why shouldn't He do the same for you? Don't believe the lie that you are destined to remain stuck where you are. Set goals now for great things you want to accomplish for God and begin working toward them.

I could have seen myself as living the homosexual lifestyle for the rest of my life. (After all, the saying is "Once gay, always gay.") But instead, by faith, I chose to see myself as a heterosexual—a husband and a father who would never seriously consider returning to my former way of life. Furthermore, I saw myself as someone who could serve God in a significant way despite my past failings. I imagined myself as a musician and a songwriter helping others worship the great God of heaven. These are goals I have accomplished.

Whatever swamp you feel you are stuck in, up ahead is a high place where the view is marvelous. Dream with God about getting there. It won't be easy, and the path may be long. But if you persevere, you will get there.

Take your first step now.

Truthstone
2 Samuel 21:20-22; 1 Chronicles 20:6-7
Jeremiah 29:11-14

A Look Inside
1. What messages have I heard in my head telling me that I can never escape the clutches of the sin or personal problem I am facing?
2. What will it take for me to turn the corner and start believing that my current giant will not always be in my life?
3. What dreams has God already given me for the future?

4. What goals am I capable of setting right now—and starting to work on?

"Even in Their Sleep..."
This evening, ask God to begin filling your mind with images of the kind of future He would like you to have.

GIANT KILLERS

Sin is like a giant
Evil and defiant
Always standing in our way
But we can defeat him
Anytime we meet him
We can face our foe and say
Hey, hey, hey
You are standing in our way
Victory is ours this day, for…

> *Giant killers, we are strong*
> *We are overcomers*
> *Giant killers, we are mighty in Jesus*
> *Giant killers, we are strong*
> *Never giver-uppers*
> *Giant killers, we are following Jesus Christ*

We have many weapons
All the pow'r of heaven
We are mighty when we praise
Giants cannot stand
Against the Father's hand
They tremble when they hear us say
Hey, hey, hey
Jesus is the only way
Victory is His this day

Putting on the armor of the Spirit
Putting on the armor of the Lord
When the giant comes, we will not fear it
For we know the One who won the war
Throw the stone of faith at the giant
Throw it 'til the giant's dead
See the mighty fall of the giant
Then cut off the giant's head and say
Hey, hey, hey
I told you get out of my way
For victory is ours this day

PART

III

THE STONE
OF IDENTITY
IN CHRIST

ELEVEN

Who Am I?

Who am I?" It is one of the most frequently asked questions in the world, yet the answer is seemingly one of the hardest to attain.

I meet people all the time who have no clue as to who they are, what their truest identity is, what their purpose in life may be. It is these same people who seem to struggle most with the day-to-day problems of life, many unable to do anything more than survive. The very thing that should bring them the most joy—understanding their identity and reason for existence—in a sense becomes one of the greatest giants they will ever encounter. If they cannot first face this giant with some measure of success, they cannot hope to do anything more than cope with, rather than run with, the life they were meant to live.

Shame is a terrible foe that those with sin or a spiritual problem in their lives must face. Images of failure in the past flood the memory. Words of condemnation rain down mentally. This Goliath giant makes a person think that who he is, at the core of his being, is a sinner (see chapter 6).

The stone required to slay this giant is the stone of our identity in Christ. Yes, we are born sinners. But if we have trusted in Christ, we are redeemed children of God, having been transformed at a fundamental level. God sees us not as covered in shame but as clothed with the righteousness of Christ. This is a truth that each of us must learn and then relearn as often as necessary.

Because of the nature of my past (my healing from homosexuality), this giant often confronts me in dramatic and difficult ways.

On the four-month anniversary of September 11, 2001, I was invited to New York City to minister to people there. From my perspective, God healed a lot of wounded, grieving hearts that weekend, and many people made life-changing decisions to follow after Christ. Many also found freedom from soul-consuming giants and made decisions to walk out of all types of sexual perversion. I returned home with a heart full of joy and gratitude that the Lord had allowed me to take part in such a glorious and humbling weekend of ministry.

But just a few days after my return, I knew something was up when I began receiving phone calls from friends asking me if I was okay. It was then I discovered that our local newspaper had run a feature article on the Op-Ed page in which the editor presented a "different" view of what had taken place on my trip to New York. (Why the paper couldn't simply print the facts about my trip, I don't know.) The impression I had as I read this scathing article was that homosexuals did not need or even want to be delivered from homosexuality and that there was, in fact, no justifiable reason for trying to rescue them from this "orientation." The article not only ridiculed me but blatantly attempted to discredit my personal story of deliverance from homosexuality. Like a giant who came taunting me (how could I ever have the same advantage as the editor of the paper, who controls what gets printed?), this verbal criticism called into question who I was. And the attack did not end there.

Over the next few weeks, the paper printed several letters to the editor in which local citizens agreed with what the editor had said about me. These were all people who believe that homosexuality can be a normal and acceptable part of life. Some of them went even further than the editor in condemning my work and ministry—my very self.

To have one's character called into question on a private level is one thing, but to have that happen in a public manner is quite another. Even when one knows the truth, such public scorn can weigh on the soul, and my soul began to grow heavy as I read the letters of criticism. In one particular letter to the editor, the writer called me a "hypocrite" and stated that "people such as Jernigan hate you, yet they do it under the guise that they care about you and want to help you." Another letter called my approach to ministry "a great gimmick that has helped him sell his music…" and went on to say that "his softly spoken story about being 'cured' from homosexuality…stirs the audience into forking out the money for his tapes." One of my favorite quotes was that I needed to "get a life."

How did this make me feel? I was already used to being attacked because of my story of freedom, and I regularly receive letters and e-mails telling me that I have obviously never been gay, that I will one day "be back," and that I am simply bisexual and living out of my heterosexual identity. Although these kinds of remarks hurt to some extent, they do not carry the sting that public ridicule does when the giant of shame comes against me. But the statements in the newspaper were deeply hurtful to me. I was tempted to give up and give in to feelings of worthlessness as a minister and as a human being. I didn't even want to go out in public for fear of what others might say or do. In the privacy of my own heart, though, I had to make a choice about what sort of response my heavenly Father would want me to make.

My first reaction was to lash out, but the Holy Spirit quickly reminded me that this was not to be my response. My response was to be one of love and grace, born out of the depths of my truest identity. I was not to defend myself. I was not to try to make myself look good by making a public statement. I was simply to rest in the truth of my identity and to trust my Father to defend me.

What did I do specifically? I reminded myself that my identity rests solely upon the truth of who my Father says I am. The harsh words of others do not determine who I am. Misguided perceptions of my ministry do not determine who I am. Feelings of fear and rejection do not determine who I am. Past failures, present feelings, persistent temptations—none of these determine who I am. I am who my Father says I am.

I was bought by the redeeming blood of Jesus Christ. I belong to God. He calls me His child. Once I was born again, nothing could ever negate that truth. And once I learned to rest in that knowledge, even the spears of mockery and scorn and rejection could not pierce my holy armor, given by God.

As I rested in the truth, an amazing thing began to happen. People I had never met began to write letters to the editor on my behalf. These were either people whose lives had been touched by the music born out of my struggles or people who just felt called to stand up for one of God's children. Letter after letter appeared. How could I stay hurt or depressed when God so openly moved to express His love for me?

What did I learn (or relearn)? I can trust my God, and I can take up the stone of my identity in Christ and rest in who He says I am, no matter how many giants rise up against me.

You can do the same.

Truthstone
Ephesians 2:1-9
Colossians 2:9-15

A Look Inside
1. What does the Goliath giant of shame say I am?
2. Who does my Father say I am, in response to this giant?

3. What will it take for me to really have confidence in my identity in Christ?

"Even in Their Sleep…"
Ask the Holy Spirit to flood your mind with the truth of who your heavenly Father says you are. Then rest in that truth all night.

TWELVE

Not in Someone Else's Armor

B efore the young David went out to meet Goliath face to face (or face to belly, perhaps), he was encouraged to wear the armor of another.

> Saul dressed David in his own tunic. He put a coat of armor on him and a bronze helmet on his head. David fastened on his sword over the tunic and tried walking around, because he was not used to them.
>
> "I cannot go in these," he said to Saul, "because I am not used to them." So he took them off. Then he took his staff in his hand, chose five smooth stones from the stream, put them in the pouch of his shepherd's bag and, with his sling in his hand, approached the Philistine. (1 Samuel 17:38-40)

Was David crazy for taking off such fine armor lent him by a king? Had he lost his mind? Merely by virtue of Goliath's being three to four feet taller, David was, in a human sense, outmanned. Add to the difference in stature the fact that Goliath was clothed in armor and carrying massive weapons, and you have the makings of a disaster.

David was not crazy, and he knew what he was doing. He had been clothed in armor that had been created for and suited to another.

So David, rather than being made more confident, had become encumbered by something never meant for him. The armor would hinder him instead of help him.

How often do we walk around encumbered by things that were never meant for us to "wear"? I would have to guess that all of us have those in-someone-else's-armor moments, whether or not we want to admit it. Looking back on my life, I sometimes find it easier to see how I "used to be" rather than to admit that, just perhaps, I am still wearing things that I was never meant to wear.

When I was a boy in grade school, other boys labeled me a "sissy" because I played the piano and could be emotional and sensitive. Since that is how others perceived me, I began to believe I really was a sissy. You already know what the ultimate effect of that self-perception was.

Another trait that surfaced when I was young was a tendency to respond to others in anger. While much of my anger arose because I felt used and wounded by people, the truth was, I responded angrily whenever I did not get my way. At such times, especially when I was still quite young, my mom would say, "That's just the Bristol coming out," referring to my great-grandparents, who evidently had a reputation for temper. What my mom meant was, "That's just the way he is; he can't help it." Again, I believed what others said—I could not help my temper.

Even as recently as two years ago, an outburst of anger revealed that there were still bits of that "old" self-perception creeping around in my soul. On one occasion I responded in anger to my wife in front of a group of friends. Though I did not recognize it at that moment, my reaction to Melinda was quite uncalled for and was deeply hurtful to her.

Thankfully, my good friends Chuck and Kathy, who had witnessed my lapse, took me aside and reminded me that the way in which I had responded to my wife was not in agreement with who

God says I am. Their perspective helped me repent of my sin, put off the vestige of anger, and replace it with the reality of who I am as a man of peace. The result? Deeper levels of honesty and intimacy with my wife and everyone else involved.

When Jesus set me free and I was reborn, I had to come to terms with the truth as God sees truth. The old Dennis passed away, and behold, something new has come forth. What does that mean? In simple terms, when I was young I may have been an angry young man. I may have believed I was a sissy. But when Christ gave me a new identity, I was given the opportunity to respond to life on a whole new level.

I had to get to the place where I could honestly say, "I used to be an angry person, but that is no longer who I am. My Father has given me a brand-new identity, one that tells me that who I am in Christ is not an angry person. I am a man of peace and slow to anger. That is who I am."

Believing anything but the truth about who God says we are is like going into battle against the giants of life with armor that is cumbersome and of little effect against such a formidable foe as rejection, addiction, or habitual sin. Putting off the lies—the armor not meant for us—and putting on the armor of who God says we are prepares us to slay even the greatest of enemies, even the enemies the world says cannot be defeated.

I was told I could not defeat homosexuality. I chose not to wear that armor. I was told I could not defeat the perception of being effeminate. I chose not to wear that armor. I was told I was an angry person. I chose not to wear that armor. I was told I would never have an effective ministry because of my past. I chose not to wear that armor. I became a giant killer by walking in the identity God gave me. I believed who *He* says I am.

All of this may sound overly simplistic, but it is reality. And the reality of God's truth always displaces the reality we thought was "just the way I am." Tell yourself this: "I do not have to settle for second best. I can go out against the giants of my life with boldness and confidence, not because of anything I am or have done, but because of who my Father says I am and because the work has already been done through the blood of Jesus Christ."

Truthstone
Romans 8:1-4
1 Peter 2:9-10

A Look Inside
1. What armor am I currently wearing that I was never meant to wear?
2. What armor should I be wearing to face the giants of my life?
3. What are some of the lies I have believed about myself, and what are the truths of God I must put on in their place?

"Even in Their Sleep…"
In your evening prayers, ask the Lord to help you take off any ill-fitting armor and put on the armor He has made just for you.

THIRTEEN

Father Knows Best

Many times when I was younger, I thought I knew more than my parents. On everything from household chores to farm responsibilities, my parents would advise me. And since they could not seem to perceive things from my perspective, I often thought they were wrong (and I secretly wondered how they had survived so long without my wisdom). When it came to the best way to respond to life's challenges, I could see only my side of things.

Many teenagers approach their lives with at least some of the kind of reasoning I had. In most cases, they are simply trying out their skills and learning to see life from their unique perspectives. You might remember having an assurance of your own wisdom and omniscience when you were a teenager. Do you remember when you realized that your parents were not so dumb after all?

When my own children began growing up and I began pouring my life and wisdom into them, I realized that my parents just might have known what they were talking about. I knew I had things to teach my kids that they needed to know—things that weren't so different from what my parents had tried to teach me. It was then I discovered that, when I was a young man, my parents had been given the wisdom and perspective that come with time and experience.

As children or teenagers, we are not suddenly gifted with deep understanding. Such gifts come with experiencing life and responding from a correct point of view, not from the nearsightedness of a selfish young man who thinks he knows it all. We have to grow into wisdom, or at least that's the way it was with me.

As it was in my transition from young man to responsible husband and father, so it was (and is) in my transition from darkness to light in understanding my true identity in Christ.

For years I mistakenly assumed that God had made a mistake with me. Somehow He had not wanted me to be like other boys. I could play the piano. I was sensitive and emotional. And the way I had been made caused other guys to label me a sissy and to taunt me for being homosexual. God had not made me a female biologically, but I had a lot of feminine characteristics, and I did not know how to handle the gifts God had given me to share my uniqueness and His blessing of love and hope with others. Since all I could see was me, and since I responded to life from my own perspective, I could not see how God could know what He was doing with me.

When did all of that change? When I realized that in all my great wisdom and understanding, I had forgotten one thing: It was *God* who had made me, not me! Sounds too simple, doesn't it? But it's true. When God gave me a new identity—when I was born again— I decided to let Him teach me about the intended use of my giftings. I would trust Him to show me who I really was.

Here's an illustration of what I'm talking about: When we buy a new gadget—say, a digital video camera—we often do not use it to its fullest potential. We may be able to turn it on and shoot some footage, but more often than not, there are features we do not use— or do not use properly. On the way to filming the new baby or the vacation to the Ozarks, we fail to record sounds properly, use the special night-filming feature, or put in those fun titles the camera allows. Why is that? Because we haven't taken time to read the manual or call the technical support personnel to see what the manufacturer says about the proper operation of said video camera.

When Christ set me free, I decided to stop believing that I knew better than my Maker. Instead, I began to read His manual—His Word—to see what He thought about my identity. Rather than rest in contentment that at least I was alive, I decided to try to live my life to its fullest possible potential as the Manufacturer had intended.

If God had given me the mind of Christ, I wanted to learn how to think like Him. If He had feelings and He was my Father, I wanted to feel life as He felt it. If His desire was to rescue and bless others at His own expense, then I wanted to learn from Him how to do that. In a spiritual sense, I stopped my rebellious teenage ways and began to understand that just maybe my Father knows best!

I began following the Lord and learning about who He says He is. And I quickly discovered that as I sought to know Him, I began to understand who I am. When I began to find out who I was intended to be, I started to put away the improper use of my thoughts. I began to feel life from the Maker's point of view. I began to use my musical giftings and emotional sensitivity passionately for Him to tell others how much He loves them and wants to set them free.

Quite simply, I let God be the Potter, and I rested in His hands as the clay. I allowed Him to be the Good Shepherd in my life, and I rested in His arms as a precious lamb He would defend with His own life. I trusted Him as Father and began to live life as a child of the Creator of life. In all this I discovered that life really is good—and Father does know best.

Truthstone
Psalm 100:3
Isaiah 64:8
Ephesians 2:10

A Look Inside

1. In what ways do I think God made me wrong?
2. How can I serve God with my particular set of gifts, qualities, and traits?

"Even in Their Sleep..."

Ask the Lord to give you a new picture of your intended identity and giftings. Perhaps He will do so in a dream this very night.

FOURTEEN

The Uniqueness of Me

R ecently I had the opportunity to meet one of the world's greatest musicians, guitarist Phil Keaggy. We had both been invited to be part of a concert series in Durango, Colorado, hosted by Buck and Annie Herring. Getting to meet Phil and spending a little time with him, I quickly realized that this gifted man was also one of the gentlest, kindest, humblest individuals I had ever met. As I left the green room and made my way to my seat, anticipation filled my heart as well as the hearts of everyone else in the capacity crowd.

Phil proceeded to play with so much precision and dexterity that it took my breath away more than once during the evening. And I was not the only one who reacted this way. After the concert I heard many comments from people in the audience that let me know these guitar fans considered Phil a hero. But there was one comment from the crowd that stuck in my mind.

As soon as the concert was over, a young man sitting directly in front of me turned to his friends and said, "I'm going home and burning my guitar!" What did he mean? Let's put it this way: If one had come to Phil's concert believing one could really play the guitar, one just might be tempted to think otherwise after witnessing Phil's mastery of the instrument!

Following the concert I was invited to the Herring home to help celebrate Buck and Annie's thirty-third wedding anniversary. Phil and his family were staying with the Herrings that night. After we blessed

Buck and Annie and shared in a meal and wonderful fellowship, I began to say my good-byes. In the process, Phil's wife, Bernadette, told me that they would see me at my "concert" the following evening, where I planned to play my guitar as part of leading worship.

Now, you have to know something about me: I consider myself a novice guitarist, having begun playing the instrument seriously less than a year ago. As a guitarist I'm nowhere near the league in which Phil Keaggy plays. And yet, how do you think I responded to Bernadette's comment? I began to laugh and get excited, and I blurted out, "I'm going to play my guitar in front of Phil Keaggy!" I was genuinely excited.

Why would someone who was about to be humiliated because of his lack of prowess on the guitar find such humor in this? Simple. Who I am is not determined by how well I perform, whether on the guitar or in any other way. Who I am is not determined by what I perceive others may or may not think of me and my abilities. Who I am is decided by my Father. I am who *He* says I am. Any talents or giftings I may have are meant to help me communicate my heart and my identity with Him and with others. Nothing more, nothing less.

Would Phil Keaggy agree with me? I'm sure he would. When I shared with Phil what the young man said about burning his guitar, Phil responded (this is a Jernigan paraphrase), "I would have told him to keep playing and that his worth is not decided by what I think."

On the night I led worship, Phil and his wife (along with my heroes Buck and Annie and Matthew Ward) were there, and I played my guitar. Feebly? Yes. With all my heart? No doubt. I played with all the confidence in the world, knowing full well that I would never play like Phil Keaggy. I played confidently because I knew my Father would be blessed in my simple yet honest expression of my love for Him. I played confidently because that is what a child of God does. I played confidently because of the realization of who and whose I am.

Don't get me wrong. I want to get better at playing the guitar. But

I will not let the magnitude of Phil's talent discourage me. Quite the contrary. Seeing the master play gives me a mark to shoot for.

I want to be like Phil Keaggy as a musician and in heart, just as I want to be like my Father, who is the Master Redeemer, Master Healer, Master Comforter, Master Blesser. Will I ever be those things at God's level? No, but I have something to shoot for. I want to be like my Father, and I'm never discouraged if I don't attain His level of mastery. I know He loves me no matter what, and this motivates me to be like Him as I minister to others.

When I began playing my guitar years ago, it was to accompany myself as I sang over my children while they were falling asleep at night. When I was injured a year ago (Achilles tendon rupture) and could not walk, I began to practice my guitar seriously as a means of overcoming depression and spending more time with my children. As my skills increased, I began using the guitar in "living-room ministry." As others would express a need for ministry, I would take up my guitar and sing over them.

One thing I have learned to do in whatever way I express my heart is to be the same person on stage or in public as I am in my living room. Whether I sing or play for one person or sing or play for thousands, nothing changes. I am confident of who my Father says I am, and I live (and play) accordingly.

God made each of us unique. He made only one Phil Keaggy, and He made only one Dennis Jernigan. The same God made both. Why would I devalue someone God calls valuable—including me?

When I first envisioned ministering in music years ago, I wanted to be like Keith Green. When Keith died, I wanted to be the next Keith Green. But the Lord quickly intervened in my thought process with these words: "Dennis, I don't need another Keith Green. I have one already. I needed a Dennis Jernigan, so I made you. I want you to be who I called you to be."

We are each uniquely created with individual characteristics and giftings that are intended to be used to commune with God, to bring Him glory, and to help lead others into a relationship with Him. We will know true freedom and confidence when we learn to value the uniqueness God has placed within each of us.

There is not another you out there. Be the you God has called you to be. Be a master of expressing God's greatness through the unique blessing of *your* identity.

‹———

Truthstone
Psalm 139:13-18
Isaiah 49:1-3

A Look Inside
1. In what ways do I get discouraged because others seem more gifted than I?
2. What lies have I believed about myself? What truth do I need to put on in the place of these lies?
3. How can I accept and value the uniqueness God has given me?

"Even in Their Sleep…"
Tonight, ask the Holy Spirit to cover you like a warm blanket with the truth of how much He values your unique identity.

MIGHTY MAN OF VALOR

Let no temptation define who you'll be
No present feeling, no past failures—you're redeemed
No weapon formed against you can ever reach as far
As the depth that I've redeemed you
Just be who the Father says you are
Just because a battle seems never to end
Doesn't mean you're losing
Just means you've something to defend

And child, you must remember
Who you are called to be
A mighty man of valor
No matter what, you have the victory

> *Take up the stone of faith*
> *And put that giant down*
> *Take up the sword of the Spirit*
> *Take back that stolen ground*
> *And lift your praise to the Father*
> *Who gives you victory*
> *You are a mighty man of valor*
> *A child of God, victorious, redeemed*

Knowing Christ is worth the battle
That is waged against your mind
With each giant you've defeated
Seems four more come right behind

Fight the fight and do not waver
And warrior, run the race
Mighty warrior, overcome
You win the fight by trusting in His grace

PART

IV

THE STONE
OF DIVINE
PERSPECTIVE

FIFTEEN

God's-Eye View

Last Christmas season my younger children came up with the idea of sleeping on the floor beside the Christmas tree on Christmas Eve. I had no objection to their plan—until they started begging me to sleep there with them.

Immediately I began to imagine how cold and hard the floor would feel. I began to think about how the glow of the tree lights would keep me awake. I was certain I would not be able to get any rest with all the distractions around the tree. So I told my kids they were welcome to sleep on the floor if they wanted to, but I would not be joining them. What I did not tell them was that I was certain they would not be able to get to sleep on the floor any more than I would.

I was wrong. No sooner had their heads hit their pillows than the twins, Asa and Ezra, were fast asleep, and snoozing right along with them was older sister Raina. How could my expectation have been so far from the truth?

The answer came when I decided to look at this sleeping arrangement from the viewpoint of my children. I got down on the floor with them, putting myself in the attitude of a child, and it took me only a few seconds to begin to feel the sense of expectancy my children had as they lay beneath the tree. Christmas was coming! In my childlike excitement, I began to dream of gifts and wonder what might be waiting beneath the tree for me.

Instead of being kept awake by the colorful lights, I was reduced to a state of wonder and awe as I contemplated the beauty of the season. I found myself suddenly restful and relaxed—and not the least bit uncomfortable on the hardwood floor. And the cold? What cold? I was warmed by the grandeur and the glory that penetrated the night as the light actually made me feel secure and at peace.

A change of perspective can make all the difference. That's true not just with a dad lying down to look at a Christmas tree from a child's perspective. It's true in the struggles we face in our spiritual lives as well.

When overcome by the pressures of circumstances or everyday existence, we often have tunnel vision. We see only that we are swamped by pain or overwhelmed by stress or shaken by temptation, and we believe that no one could possibly understand or help us in our battle. Discouragement creeps in, and we think our lives will never get any better. That's the giant Ishbi-Benob rising to challenge us (see chapter 7).

If we want freedom and victory, we must refuse to give in to that kind of discouragement. We have to look at the giants in our lives from some perspective other than our own. A great place to begin is by discovering God's perspective concerning our particular circumstances. The stone useful against the Ishbi-Benob giant of discouragement, then, is the stone of divine perspective.

One of the most profound statements of a proper life perspective I have ever made to myself is this: *He is God; I am not.* In other words, when confronted with the enormity of a giant in my life, I need to remember that my point of view is not the only one. In fact, my point of view will probably be skewed at least a little bit.

If God is who He says He is, then He has all knowledge and all power and does not miss a thing. To put my giants down, I need to step outside myself and my circumstances and try to see them from God's vantage point. From His perspective, impossibilities are suddenly made possible. Insufferable pain is suddenly made bearable. Failure is suddenly rendered glorious. Questions of "Why?" and "Why me?" are suddenly answered by the grace to endure that is found only from God's point of view.

We need but crawl into the lap of our heavenly Father and learn to trust Him and His perspective on what is best for us. His Word tells us that His ways are higher than ours and His thoughts are higher than ours (see Isaiah 55:8-9). If He is God and yet we constantly try to decide what is in our own best interests (mainly our desire to get out of difficult circumstances) rather than allowing Him to carry us through, then we are usurping His authority and place in our lives. We are acting as gods on our own behalf, and that will never result in victory over the giants in our lives.

Whatever trial we find ourselves in, whatever predicament we face, whatever fear or pain we must deal with, one of the most effective weapons in our spiritual arsenal is the ability to view each circumstance from the Father's perspective. This doesn't mean our circumstances aren't real or hurtful; it just means we aren't defeated by them. And getting to this place of trust makes us candidates for deep outpourings of God's grace in the midst of our trials. Remember, grace is the power only God can give to carry us through to victory in spite of the giants we may face in life.

He is God; I am not. That truth brings levels of peace and rest we never thought possible, even when the world seems to be falling apart around us.

He is God.

Truthstone
Isaiah 55:8-9
Ephesians 3:20-21

A Look Inside

1. What circumstances in my life could I face better if I were to see them from God's point of view?
2. In what areas of my life am I currently acting like my own god, as if I am in charge? How can I get off the throne and allow God to sit there?
3. How can I gain God's perspective on my problems?

"Even in Their Sleep…"

Ask the Holy Spirit to let you see God's perspective on a current problem in your life.

SIXTEEN

The Importance of Truth

S in always has self at the center. When we are engaged in sin, we are focused on our problems, our feelings, our schemes for doing what we think best for ourselves. We are not looking to God and His desires for our lives. We are on the throne of our lives, so no one else can help us.

If you have a giant in your life, I expect this pattern sounds familiar to you.

But what if I could show you a better vantage point from which to evaluate your life, one from which you could see the reality of the danger in which you have placed your mind, your emotions, and even your physical body? Would you be willing to step down from the throne of your heart long enough to see what life might be like with someone else on the throne—someone with the power, love, and authority to make life-giving changes to the kingdom of your life? If so, read on. If not, I cannot help you.

I am going to share with you more of my own experience with homosexuality. I realize that your giant may look very different from mine, yet I believe that what I am about to share can be applied to any sin in any person's life.

When I was involved in homosexuality, I desperately wanted to put an end to that behavior in my life. Yet I understood enough to realize that underneath the level of my behavior was another level— the level of my feelings. I had been bombarded by feelings of rejection from my father and other men, and these feelings had worked themselves out in my life in the form of homosexual behavior. But why did I have those feelings?

It is really quite a simple explanation. In fact, it sounds *too* simple. But it is the truth. My problem? I finally realized what it was: a wrong belief system.

Below the level of my behavior was the level of my emotions, but still more basic was the level of my thinking. My sense of what was true was flawed. In my mind I believed that I was an unworthy person who deserved to be rejected. So I interpreted other people's behavior as rejection…and therefore felt rejected by men…and therefore acted as one cast out of normal manhood.

Healing could begin in my life only when I accepted the real truth. God loved me no matter what. Men may have rejected me, but He never did. My identity and my value lay in Him. Through His power, I was capable of normal functioning as a man.

To overcome my homosexual behavior, I had to do several things. I had to come to a point where I either stepped down from the throne or stayed there. To stay there would have meant that Christ had no power to rule in my life because I had usurped that power. I also had to accept the truth that God's Word is true—regardless of what my feelings told me, regardless of what my past experiences told me, regardless of what the popular culture told me, regardless of what any other voice would try to say. It was at this point—the point where DJ was dethroned—that God was able to demonstrate His power in my life.

Simply put, a wrong belief system leads to wrong feelings. Wrong feelings lead to wrong behavior. This is the way to destruction, so it would stand to even worldly reason that reversing this flow would lead to constructive behavior. In other words, a right belief system leads to right feelings, which leads to constructive behavior.

I struggled with homosexuality for many years. I did everything in my power to not walk in that behavior. But as I tried to behave the right way, I was devastated every time I fell back into the wrong behavior. After a while, I simply accepted the "fact" that this must be the way I am. Because I believed this was my identity, rather than considering the possibility that God might have another idea, my wrong belief system kept me stuck in a vicious cycle of destruction.

I believed a lie. The lie led me to believe I really was rejected. My need for acceptance and affirmation from men led me to seek out that affirmation and acceptance for myself through homosexual behavior. That behavior, in turn, led me to reaffirm my identity as a homosexual. The reaffirmation led to renewed feelings of rejection and, again, to wrong behavior. Over and over and over. I honestly did believe I was born that way. But what a happy day when I realized the truth!

We often quote John 8:32: "You will know the truth, and the truth will set you free." But what does that mean? We can talk about the truth and try to perform the truth, but all we get in the process is a performance—and more bondage. The word for "know," in this instance, is the same word used when Mary was told by the angel that she would conceive and give birth to a son, Jesus. "How shall this be," Mary asked the angel, "seeing I know not a man?" (Luke 1:34, KJV). In other words, Mary was saying she had never had an intimate experience with a man. Since this had never occurred, she could not—in natural terms—conceive or realize a birth. So it is with truth.

How can truth set us free if we never have a personal and intimate experience with that truth? It cannot. In order for us to find the freedom truth offers, we must first have a personal experience with that truth. We must get honest with ourselves and with our God. You see, honesty is always the first step we must take toward truth. And we cannot have a personal experience with God's truth if we do not accept it as *the* truth. In other words, I would never have gotten to freedom if I had chosen to disregard the truth. Either God is God or He is not. Either His Word is true or it is not. If we do not accept God's Word as truth, that truth can never set us free, because we do not have personal experience with something we give no credence to.

If our God is almighty God, and if His Word has been given to us as a road map to life, we must accept His Word as the foundation from which our belief system operates. Unless we get to the place where we lay aside our personal agendas in favor of His, then He and His Word cannot help us. As long as we operate from our own perspective (experiences, feelings, thought processes, and so on), His perspective and power are blocked from our view, and we feel threatened when God's perspective is presented to us. To live our lives apart from His perspective is to create an illusion of life. Anything that does not have as its foundation the truth that God calls truth is merely a distortion of the facts and is laced with deceit.

We must line up on the side of truth. When we say, "I can't save myself," then God is free to say, "I can!" We must put on the truth and allow it to be the foundation from which we live our lives. Every truthless area of our lives is filled with darkness.

The bottom line for freedom? Know the truth, and it will set you free. Get off the throne and let Him reign there. Let Him be God and allow the Creator to be creative in your life. A right belief system—the truth as God sees it—leads to healthy emotions. Healthy emotions lead to healthy behavior.

Truthstone
John 14:5-7
Romans 12:1-2
1 Corinthians 2:14-16

A Look Inside
1. How are my actions, feelings, and perceptions of truth interrelated?
2. How can I exchange false "truth" for true truth?

"Even in Their Sleep..."
This evening, ask the Holy Spirit to show you the areas in which you have been believing a lie and to lead you into the truth.

SEVENTEEN

When We Don't Understand

When I was thirteen years old, my Grandmother Jernigan died. She had been a confidante for me. She often called me in from my daily chores in the winter and encouraged me to warm up my hands at the piano. She taught me about God's love and how to listen for His voice. She was always in my corner. She understood me. But then she died. And I asked the Lord, "Why?"

Six years ago my sister-in-law Sandy lost her six-year-old nephew, Jordan, in an accident. Jordan's parents, along with the rest of us, wondered why God would allow this tragedy to happen to such a young child with such a loving family.

One of the most profound questions of my own life has been "Why did You allow homosexuality to be a part of my life, Lord?" Having suffered through so much to get to a place of healing, I wondered why God had not stepped in and prevented that pain from becoming part of my life.

I realized at last that I had many unanswered questions about my past. Because some of those memories involved hurtful or shameful things, I was often bogged down with despair and depression over what I had experienced, wondering where the Lord had been when bad things were happening to me, where He had been when I needed a way of escape from my temptations, where He had been when I needed protection.

One day I finally grew tired of the cycle of depressing thoughts and despair, so I decided to do something about it. I made a list of many of those times when I thought God had not been there for me. Then I prayed for the Holy Spirit to show me the reality of the situation.

Soon after I made the list, God began to answer my prayers for redemption in these hurtful areas. One example occurred after I led a worship service in my hometown.

A gray-haired lady named June Smith approached me and asked, "Isn't it wonderful how your Grandmother Jernigan's prayers have been answered?"

"I don't know what you're talking about," I replied.

"Do you remember when you would come into your grandmother's house and play the piano?"

"I remember those times well. They are some of my most precious memories."

"Well, didn't you know? Your grandmother told me how she would stand behind you as you practiced the piano at her house each day and would ask God to use you mightily in His kingdom to lead in music and worship. Then she would come to our weekly prayer gathering and ask the rest of us to agree with her in prayer on your behalf. And He has answered our prayers!"

June added that she and several of my grandmother's other prayer partners were still praying for me.

Instantly the Holy Spirit showed me the truth of God's perspective. Not only had He *not* abandoned me, but He had even multiplied my grandmother's prayers for me—and they continue to this day!

That evening something lifted from my soul. No longer would I allow a hurtful memory to keep me locked up in depression or despair. I began to look forward to seeing each situation from God's perspective because it meant I would no longer have to be weighed down by the burdens of those events.

I asked the Lord to show me where He was when I was being victimized. When I was five, a man had exposed himself to me in a public restroom. I had run away from him, but it made me wonder, *Why did he pick me to do that to? What is wrong with me?* Years later, as a young man, I was betrayed by an older mentor who wanted to use me sexually. It threw me into despairing that I would ever get free of homosexuality. Where was God when such things were happening?

He reminded me that He had protected me and gotten me this far.

I asked the Lord to show me where He had been when I had been tempted with certain sins. During the period when I was getting deeper and deeper into homosexuality, it had seemed as if I could never resist the pull of that lifestyle (or "deathstyle," as I like to call it). Couldn't God have kept me from the temptation?

God reminded me that He had been there, calling to me with the way of escape—and that I had not had ears to hear and had not received the grace to overcome my sin.

I could go on giving you examples, but I'm sure you recognize the same pattern in your own life. When we look back, God was there. God is always there.

Let me assure you of this, my friend: The stones that hang around our necks and weigh us down can be cut away and used to build an altar to the God who makes a way where we see none. Now even my past failures and the subsequent shame have been replaced by truth, and those very things are being used to bring glory to the God who delivers those who are willing to see life from His point of view.

If you are reading this book, you will understand my reasoning. If God had not allowed me to take this path, I would not know how to lead others out. If I had never known the sorrow of such bondage, I would never know the gladness of true freedom. God knew I would respond the way I did to His call to freedom and that I would be inclined to tell others about all He has done for me. God knew you would need to read this story.

Two instances from the life of Christ confirm what I am sharing with you. As Jesus walked with His disciples one day, He saw a man who had been blind from birth. His disciples asked, "Rabbi, who sinned, this man or his parents, that he was born blind?"

"Neither this man nor his parents sinned," Jesus said, "but this happened so that the work of God might be displayed in his life" (John 9:3). Jesus healed the man's blindness, causing many to reconsider what they knew about God.

One of my favorite passages of Scripture, the story of Lazarus, bears out the same truth about glorifying God:

> Now a man named Lazarus was sick. He was from Bethany, the village of Mary and her sister Martha.... So the sisters sent word to Jesus, "Lord, the one you love is sick."
>
> When he heard this, Jesus said, "This sickness will not end in death. No, it is for God's glory so that God's Son may be glorified through it." (John 11:1-4)

Again, Jesus amazed many by raising up Lazarus.

My healing has come as I have focused on dreadful episodes of my life from God's perspective instead of from my own narrow perspective. From His point of view, bad situations bear the fruit of hope. In His way of thinking, even the things Satan intended for harm and destruction bring peace and healing and life.

Why does God allow bad things? Look at the thousands of lives that have been touched just by my little story of God's grace and love, and tell me it was not worth it. God's glory begets more of all He is. Even from our greatest failures, He is able to bring forth the greatest victories. From death He brings life. From despair He brings hope. From depression He brings joy. God allows bad things, but His grace is sufficient, and the glory is worth it!

Are you ready to look at your life from God's vantage point? The view is freeing. I guarantee you'll like what you see.

Truthstone
John 9
John 11:1-44
John 13:37-38; 18:17,25-27; 21:15-19

A Look Inside
1. What wounds or past events make me feel as if God has forsaken or abandoned me? What questions do I need to ask Him to find His perspective in these areas?
2. If I were to build an altar to show that my past hurts and failures have been cut away, what would it look like?
3. How might God be working right now to bring glory to Himself through my life?

"Even in Their Sleep..."
Ask the Lord to increase your faith to believe that He is working to bring good out of the sadness, struggle, and disappointment in your life.

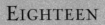

EIGHTEEN

What Will God Do Next?

A few years ago my friend Paul Brothers was at a horse show with his daughter Jesse when he noticed a sign posted on the arena bulletin board. The sign advertised a large home for sale. At first he thought, *Too bad it's not near Dennis and Melinda. They need a larger home for their family.* Then he moved on.

A little while later, curiosity got the better of him, and he went back to check out the location of the house. *Muskogee, Oklahoma? Why, this home is only sixteen miles from where Melinda and Dennis are now living.*

Paul called us the next day to tell us about the home. We went to look at it, and without dragging the tale out any longer, I can tell you that today we live in that home on 113 acres. And we are still only sixteen miles from my folks. Our finding that house was an answer to prayer in more ways than one. Awesome!

But that was not everything. Here is the rest of the story.

About four months ago, Paul called with some bad news. Jake, a beautiful horse that Jesse had ridden in many equestrian competitions, had been diagnosed with an incurable disease of the muscles. Jesse would not be able to ride him anymore. In fact, the veterinarian was suggesting that Paul consider putting Jake down.

Jesse was devastated, and Paul was concerned on her behalf. His question for me was this: "Would it be possible for Jake to live out his days on the Jernigan farm rather than me having to put my daughter through the trauma of putting her horse to sleep?"

As Paul was speaking, I was thinking about all he has meant to me. God had brought him into my life years earlier to teach me about godly relationships between men. Paul has always been faithful to care about and pray for me and my family. He is an eternal friend. And so, before he had even finished his request, I knew the answer to his question.

On the day Paul and Jesse brought Jake to our farm, there was sadness in the air. Jesse knew she would never again feel the wind rushing through her hair as she galloped her Jake across the fields. She would not get to see him every day as she had been used to. Things would never be the same.

Yet, at the same time, we felt joy. Jesse would not be entirely parted from her beloved horse. Jake had been given a new lease on life. And he would not be alone—six Jernigan horses would see to that! The goodness of God was obvious to all.

God knows.

God had known that I would need a friend. God had known that Melinda and I would need a bigger house for our nine children. God had known that Jake would get sick. And God had known that there would be comfort for Jesse and a wonderful place for Jake to live out his days in peace, because He had engineered it all.

One result of having a proper perspective—that is, a perspective that sees life in its many facets, both good and bad, from God's point of view—is celebration. With such a perspective, the good times are really good and even the bad times seem valuable for the amount of maturity we gain through dealing with them.

Today I am able to celebrate the freedom I have gained from viewing my life from God's vantage point. When I see the loss of a loved one from God's point of view, I have hope in knowing I will see that loved one again. I don't have to walk around playing the "What if?" game and dealing with regrets. When I view a shattered dream or a broken vision from God's perspective, I have hope in realizing that He knows what is best for me. I don't have to be bogged down with despair, because I have been set free to explore new opportunities to be creative with God. Even when I fall into sin, I have hope in knowing that God forgives and restores. I don't have to walk around in the bondage of shame and guilt, because I know my God loves me and accepts me no matter what. Seeing myself from God's perspective sets me free to willingly receive His love and follow Him with my whole heart.

Sometimes we don't see the hand of God until everything He has been doing suddenly falls into place. But looking at such circumstances as we experienced with Jesse and Jake offers proof of the creativity and splendor of life from God's perspective. When we look at circumstances this way, living gets pretty exciting. We think, *I can't wait to see what's next* and *I can't wait to see how Father fixes this mess.*

God's perspective is grand and full of joy. He loves to bless His children. He knows our hurts and He knows our needs. He knows we need Him. He knows.

Truthstone
Genesis 50:15-20
Isaiah 43:18-21
Romans 8:18-30

A Look Inside
1. How good am I at exchanging my perspective for God's?
2. Why did God allow me to be born to the parents He did? Why did He allow me to grow up where and how I did? In what ways do I see His hand in the particular giftings He has given me?

3. What past hurtful or unpleasant memories would I like to look
   back at from God's perspective? What might I then see?

"Even in Their Sleep…"
Go to bed tonight thanking God for the creative ways in which He
has engineered, and is still engineering, your life.

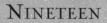

NINETEEN

What You've Been Given

Many times we succumb to the lies of the Enemy by focusing on what we don't have. I don't know what lacks in life you regret, but I could say (and have said) things like these: "I didn't have music lessons." "I didn't have a normal experience with men as a boy." "I don't have all the resources others do." "I don't have the time to do all I want." "I don't have the right look to be a successful musician." The list could be endless.

As I have already stated, I have asked why God allowed me to struggle with homosexuality. The reality is, I did not choose to be born with the giftings, sensitivities, and emotions that are part of my experience. I did not choose the way I was brought up. I did not even choose to be tempted by homosexuality. Yes, when I was old enough to understand what I was doing, I did have a choice about how I would respond to those temptations. Yet God still allowed me to go through that experience. Why?

I recently heard my pastor say that God is a God of risk. He knows all and is all powerful, yet He chose to give us the ability to choose. He gave us free will. He did not create us to be holy zombies or spiritual clones or sacred robots. He wants us to love Him because we want to love Him, not because we have to. He is willing to risk our rejection because His great love requires such risk.

God was willing to risk losing me to homosexuality because He knew I could also choose to seek Him for healing—and then tell others about all He had done. He was willing to risk my use of the musical and emotional gifts He had given me, knowing how much I would love Elton John. He knew that if I turned to Him, I would use my gifts out of the deep gratitude I felt for His setting me free. My God chose to risk it all, and then He chose to express Himself and His love and His plan for redeeming humankind, through me! He is God; I am not. And as my friend Jack Taylor says, "I don't have the sense to make sense of God's sense."

If I had wallowed in self-pity and regret over all I had to endure to get to my healing, I would never have been able to get anything done for God. I decided early on, after my deliverance, that I would try to see the glass of my life half full rather than half empty. I would choose to live with what I had been given rather than to live by what I did not have.

Soon after Melinda and I were married, we began having children. During that period I taught school for three years, making only eight hundred dollars a month. Yet God made a way for us to survive. We had popcorn and potatoes and chose to see the plenty rather than the lack.

Following my period of teaching, I began working for a church as secretary by morning and janitor by afternoon—and worship leader after a year. Having few resources, I had (at least in my estimation) very little to work with. What was I to do?

One time I wanted to display the names of God around the auditorium, but we had no money to work with. Yet we did have a huge roll of butcher paper, and I knew how to draw and how to write in a calligraphic style. In a week's time we had ten amazing banners depicting some of the covenant names of God. The metallic paint we used and the way in which the banners hung gave the appearance of velvet and rich texture. When people saw them, we had inquiries from all over the city (and eventually, the country) as to how to make such banners.

As worship leader I often found it difficult to find songs that re-
inforced the direction in which we were heading as a church body, so
I began to ask God for songs that would encourage the truth we were
learning from His Word. He gave them, and they were a blessing to
the congregation. Soon people were asking for those songs, but I had
no way of recording them.

I had dreamed of having a recording contract (as all young musicians do) but realized the reality of that world was a far cry from what
my visions entailed. In light of this realization, I decided to once again
make do with what I had. I saved enough money to purchase a four-
hundred-dollar four-track recording machine, which I immediately
dubbed "studio-in-a-box." To record my first album, I set up a micro-
phone and hit Record, telling no one what we were doing. We just
worshiped God. That tape (no CDs in those days) sold around sixty
thousand copies in two years.

I immediately needed sheet music because of the demand, but I
had only a small Macintosh on which to produce music. So Melinda
and I began Shepherd's Heart Music in response to this need. If we
had chosen to give up because of our perspective—because of what
we did not have—you might not be reading this book. Who knew?
God knew.

Since 1987 we have sold more than 1.5 million units. To me, that
is an incredible number. As I shared this with my son Israel one day,
though, he reminded me, "Dad, *NSYNC sold that much in one
week." There's that perspective thing again.

My perspective? I choose to see what I have rather than what I
don't have. I can't wait to see the millions of people whose lives have
been impacted by my music and testimony in such a way that they
find themselves set free…or healed…or in heaven! I will not be limi-
ted by my limitations. God's willingness to risk my knowing Him,
coupled with His great creativity in working in my life, carries me
over, above, and beyond even my wildest dreams. Who knew?

———

Truthstone
1 Kings 17:7-16
Matthew 14:13-21
Philippians 4:13

A Look Inside

1. What areas of my life am I looking at from the perspective of what I don't have? How can I change to look at those areas from God's vantage point and the perspective of what I do have?
2. What are my limitations? Time? Money? Help? How might God express His creativity through me to overcome these limitations?

"Even in Their Sleep…"

Ask the Holy Spirit to give you a vision of how to overcome your limitations.

I Believe

I know what I know many don't believe
Jesus can really set them free
I know they won't know if they do not see
Jesus alive and well in me
Lord, live Your life through me that others might see
Your awesome love and the hope they all need
Jesus, I believe

> *You are the God of love who is faithful*
> *In stormy seas the rock that is stable*
> *When I am weak the God who is able*
> *You are my life and victory*
> *You are the God who saved me, redeeming*
> *Upon the cross forgiveness came streaming*
> *You rose again. You gave my life meaning*
> *You are my God, and this is what I believe*

This truth can break through and set people free
My life the only truth some see
I'll go, I'll follow wherever You lead
Jesus alive and well in me
You are the answer that asking hearts need
You are the answer, the truth I believe
Jesus, I believe

Lies will come against your soul
Will you stand or will you be deceived?
Lies assail. Like wind, they blow
Who you are is what your heart believes
Jesus is alive in me
Lord, this is what I believe

PART

V

THE STONE
OF INTIMACY
WITH GOD

TWENTY

Connecting with God

When by God's grace I turned away from my sin of homosexuality in 1981, fears quickly crowded in. What if people found out what I had done in the past? What if temptation arose in a form I could not resist? What if I embarrassed myself and angered God by falling back into my old sin patterns after all He had done for me? What if, what if, what if…?

It is not unusual for someone who is trying to eliminate sin or some other spiritual problem from his or her life to face multiplied fears. Under the best of circumstances, these fears are merely troubling. At worst, they can paralyze us like a toxin, keeping us from moving forward into the future filled with the freedom that God has set out before us.

Through experience I eventually discovered that my fears were *in themselves* temptations from the devil. He didn't have to get me to slip back into homosexuality; paralyzing me with fear was enough to accomplish his goal of keeping me from living fully for God. In other words, fear can be a giant in our lives. It is our Saph (see chapter 8).

The same stone that felled my Saph giant of fear will fell yours, too. It is the stone of intimacy with God. As we sink into God's loving embrace, we feel so secure in Him that every fear must flee our hearts. In the words of Scripture, "perfect love drives out fear" (1 John 4:18). And God's love is the only perfect love we'll ever know.

My fellow giant killer, we must understand intimacy with God.

We'll be looking at different aspects of this sort of intimacy over the next few chapters, and among these aspects, the most basic is having a relationship with Him. We Christians often glibly toss out such phrases as "having a personal relationship with God." But what does that really mean?

Relationship means connection. If I have relationship with my wife, then she and I must connect on emotional, mental, and physical levels. We share each other's feelings. We share each other's thoughts. And we share each other's bodies (one of my favorite things to share with her!).

As a result of the connection between my wife and me, we exchange life. And we produce life—life begets more life. Emotional freedom results for both of us. Love is laid down as a foundation. And in our case, children—nine of 'em!—have resulted as Melinda and I have exchanged life.

In any relationship, life cannot be produced if life is not exchanged. The reason so many relationships fail is because life is shared only on a physical level (the surface) or perhaps on an emotional level (the bridge from the mind to the surface). It never gets to the deeper level of the mind (our true identity).

So it is in our relationship with the Lord. We want change, so we turn to Him. But change doesn't occur because we let Him get only to the "physical" or "emotional" levels. We seek a change in our behavior, so we try to follow certain rules or jump through all the right hoops because we want the change to be seen. We seek out emotional experiences and live from one to the next until we collapse from the exhaustion of feeling our way through life.

To live like this means we "do" to exist. We perform well to be accepted. That kind of living does not lead to life.

Relationship requires real intimacy. Intimacy means letting someone see you at your deepest place, the point of who you really are. Intimacy means "into me see." I allow the Father to see into me, and then He invites me to see into Him. Such relationship requires trust and is a prerequisite to life.

If I did not allow my wife to see into my thoughts or feel my emotions with me or share my body with her, life would never occur and that relationship would die. So it is with my relationship with the Lord. If I desire life, I must seek Him intimately. I must exchange life with Him on every level.

My life must have as its foundation the right belief system. God's truth must be the place where intimacy begins. I am who He says I am. This leads to an exchange of right feelings because I now understand who He says I am. These right feelings lead to right behavior. No longer do I perform to be accepted by Him; I simply believe I am who He says I am, and I perform in a righteous manner because that is who I am.

When the Enemy whispers reminders concerning our past failures, we can either entertain them or we can choose to hear the truth. To listen to the lies of the Enemy is to practice intimacy with him, and intimacy with the Enemy always leads to our destruction and ultimate failure.

If we are ever to be giant killers, we must learn to trust God on the most intimate of levels. After all, why should we hide from the One who sees our hidden sins and continues to love us anyway? One of the ways I practice intimacy when the Enemy attacks is to cry out to God and ask Him to let me hear what *He* says about me. I love to hear Him remind me that while a certain failure may have been a reality for me at one time, that failure has been forgiven, something new has come in its place, and who He says I am is who I am. I am *not* what I have done.

If you desire freedom, seek to know God intimately. If you desire change, seek to know God intimately. If you need hope or joy or emotional healing, seek to know God intimately. Relationship is everything!

Truthstone
John 15:5-17
1 Corinthians 13:9-13
1 John 4:12-19

A Look Inside
1. What do I fear?
2. What hidden things are keeping me from enjoying deeper intimacy with Christ?
3. In what areas do I need intimacy with God?

"Even in Their Sleep…"
This evening, ask the Holy Spirit to let you see a glimpse of what your life would be like if you were free from all fear and anxiety.

When I Can't Hear God

Today I was driving down the road after having one of my all-
too-common fits of complaining to God. Here I am, someone
who has everything he really needs in life—health, family, friends, the
love of God, and more—and yet all I can see and communicate to
God is that the house is falling apart, the finances are nonexistent, the
direction of my life seems to be taking yet another turn, no one
understands me, and certainly no one cares. This all left me wondering (since I have been in this midlife "How will I ever provide for my
family?" spot for about two years now) if I had ever heard God in the
first place. I certainly felt that I could not hear Him now.

As I drove to the school my children attend to deliver a birthday
cake for my son Judah, I glanced at the sign in front of a local Christian bookstore. All it said was, "It's not about you." *Whap!* Big stone
of truth upside the head. Once again I had let some of the old giants
of insecurity sneak back into my life, and because my perspective had
been my own and not God's, I had suddenly found myself focused
upon—you guessed it!—me.

One of the best ways to hear from God when it seems that we
haven't been able to hear anything from Him is to get still. To get
quiet. So I knew that I had to quiet my own thoughts. Quiet my own
emotions. Quiet my own will and desire for personal gratification.
And wouldn't you know it? God up and speaks—with a little help

from a storefront sign that could have been designed just for me. (Somewhere up in heaven, God was laughing.)

One of the best things I have discovered to help me overcome the giants in my life is realizing that I am not here on this earth for my own pleasure and glory. I was placed here to give God pleasure and to bring Him glory. One of the biggest distractions I have found when trying to hear God's voice is my own selfishness—my focus on *me.*

I wasted years complaining that nobody loved me and that no one understood me. If I had been someone else listening to me, I would have walked the other way whenever I saw me coming. No wonder I didn't have many friends. All I thought about was me and my own needs.

In a way, the noise of my own complaining attitude, especially after I was set free and began to know better, drowned out the voice of God. Anything I allow to speak in my life with more volume than God's voice keeps me from hearing God as clearly as I should. When I first realized this truth, I became aware that I had allowed the Enemy to speak more loudly into my life than God. So what did I do?

I began to go through every area of my life and cut out the noise of anything that robbed me of hearing God's voice. Some things I kept outside of hearing range for good, such as wrong places and wrong friends. Some things I cut out until I got a better handle on them, such as too much television or even music. In fact, for ten years I did not listen to any music—Christian or secular—so that I could hear God's voice more clearly. What I discovered was a world of peace in which God was more than happy to speak, especially when my focus was on Him and others or when I came to Him in gratitude, regardless of my circumstances.

Because of all it has done for me, this is an exercise I urge on anyone who has a hunger to hear God speak. If this describes you, then

I suggest you ask yourself, "In what areas of my life can I turn down the volume?" In other words, what can you cut out of your life or cut down on or pay less attention to so that you can focus on what God is saying to you? Make all the changes it takes until God is coming through loud and clear to you.

Musicians train their ears to hear everything that's going on in a piece of music. New parents become alert to the first sound of unhappiness in the baby's room down the hall. Certain technicians and engineers have learned to pick up the sound of the one piece in a great machine that is malfunctioning. You can train your ears to hear God, too, and the best tactic for doing this is to dial down other sounds that interfere. Ultimately, our ability to hear God is based upon whether we are listening with a trusting heart, and our level of success is directly proportionate to how many other voices we are listening to.

God's Word reminds us to be still and to what? To be still and to *know that He is God* (see Psalm 46:10). Yes, He is God and we are not. Learning to be still and listen for Him is key to recognizing our place versus His, our desires versus His, our plans versus His.

It is not about us. It is about Him—all about Him.

Shh! Learn to be still and listen.

Truthstone
1 Kings 19:9-18
Psalm 46:8-10

A Look Inside
1. Am I quick to hear the voice of God, or am I slow?
2. What other noises in my life might be drowning out the voice of God? How can I tune them out?

3. When I think about God speaking, what do I imagine He sounds like? Is He angry? comforting? stern? gracious? firm?

"Even in Their Sleep..."
Ask God to help you understand what the Holy Spirit is speaking to your spirit.

TWENTY-TWO

Hearing God Speak
Your Name

Recently I took my children camping alongside a nearby river. They could not wait to get into the water and swim across the wide expanse. After all, they had heard my stories of time spent on this same river when I was a child and of how much fun my brothers and I had on the other side. I'll never forget the first time I was given permission to swim across the river when I was a boy and how liberating it felt to leave the shallows and head for the fun of the deep.

Of course, my ten-year-old boys had come to the conclusion that now was the time for them to experience that same rite of passage. So I sent them across with my blessing. As a matter of fact, I felt much joy as I watched them making their way across the river, swimming against the powerful current. They wound up being carried farther downstream than they had anticipated, but they made it across safely.

After they enjoyed a time of playing on the other side, I called them in for dinner and watched again to make sure they made it safely back to camp. Ezra compensated properly for the current this time and made the crossing in fairly quick order. Asa, on the other hand, did not do so well. The current began to take him off course, and I could tell that he was beginning to panic.

What did I do? I called out to him by name. "Asa! It's okay. I'm right here. Asa, swim toward my voice." When my little boy made it across to my waiting arms, all he could do was thank me for saving his life!

For many years I, like Asa, attempted to make it across the river of life on my own. Most of the time, because of the currents of my temptations, I was swept into places and situations far too precarious for me to handle alone. In danger of drowning in my own sense of failure and worthlessness, I felt too far gone (or too much in fear of the giants in my life) to even believe that God would desire to help me.

But when I was set free from the power of my sin and began to understand how much I had been lied to by the Enemy, I began to seek God. Namely, I sought Him through prayer and through learning to hear His voice in an intimate manner. What an exciting discovery this new intimacy in relationship was! I felt as thrilled by it as my boys were when they crossed the river that first time.

It was a revelation for me to understand that God not only loves me but also calls out to me by name. He has specific things to tell about who I am, who He is, and what He has in store for me. He has words for me that provide guidance and comfort at whatever stage of life I may find myself in. His Word tells me that, as His sheep, I can actually hear the Shepherd's voice (see John 10:27). Amazing!

So how did I learn to hear His voice? Initially, it was just as my children seek to know me: I began to ask Him questions and then wait for His answer. At first, my questions were childlike: "Father, do You love me?" I soon learned, however, that God was not afraid of any question I might ask. So I began to ask some more difficult questions. "Father, *how* do You love me?" "How can You fix the mess I have made of my life?" "How can I minister life to this person who faces physical death?" And so on.

God does not speak to me in an audible voice, as some say they have heard Him. Who knows? Maybe one day He will talk to me that way. But I have discovered that if I am paying attention, I can "hear"

Him speaking in a variety of ways. Through words in His Book that I have skimmed over many times before but that now pierce right into my heart. Through a "still, small voice" in my heart—a kind of subtle yet powerful impression. Through the encouraging words or actions of a friend. Even through the image of a little boy swimming safely into his father's arms.

In the next chapter I will be touching more on the ways we can hear God speak. My point right now is *that* we can hear God speak—and that we'll never hear Him speak unless we open ourselves up to the conversation.

You can begin at the same place I did in seeking a relationship of intimacy with God. Ask Him questions and listen to hear His response. Of course, you need to be prepared for God to answer in ways you may not desire! After all, He is God and you are not. But His answers are always right and true, and hearing and living by them draws you nearer to Him, to the place where your fears are banished.

If you want to be a giant killer, you must learn the power of prayer. And prayer, of course, being conversation, is both talking and listening. You probably know how to talk to God just fine. Most of us fall down in the area of listening to what God has to say in return. So work on your skills in listening. God has words just for you, and I wouldn't want you to miss a single one.

What I have discovered above all in listening to God over a period of many years is that even though I still must face times of swimming against the currents of temptation and battling the giants of my thought life, I can trust that God is with me. He calls out my name to let me know I am not alone and gives me a place to look for direction as I learn to detect the nuances and whispers of His voice speaking to me.

How do we know God is there? By learning to hear His voice moment by moment.

Truthstone
1 Samuel 3:1-10
John 10:22-30

A Look Inside
1. What would it mean to me to hear God calling my name?
2. What would I like to hear God saying to me right now?
3. What are some questions I would like to ask the Father?

"Even in Their Sleep…"
Tonight, in your prayer time, ask the Father to let you hear something good about yourself.

Ways of Hearing

Melinda and I have nine children, which means we are raising nine unique individuals, all with their own perspective on life and their own way of processing what they hear. It has been in watching my children grow, and then in trying to communicate with them in ways that build them up in their own identities and giftings, that I have learned much about how God speaks to me. His communication to me is right for how He has created me, and it may not be the same as the way He communicates to others.

I am a guy who gets impressions of what I believe God may be saying to me. It may be a thought, or it may be a kind of pressure in the core of my being. I can't exactly explain it to you, but I've become comfortable with the thought that this is a primary way God has wired me to hear His voice.

For you, hearing the voice of God may take on an entirely different character. Maybe you'll hear an audible voice. Maybe you'll see signs in nature that point you to what you need to know. It could be many things; I don't know what it will be for you. But I do know that just as we have many ways of speaking to one another on a human level, so, too, God has created many and varied ways for us to speak to and hear from Him.

My main desire is to let you know how simple communication with God can be—that we can hear His voice if we learn to listen. I also hope to stir up in you a desire to seek God in deeper and more creative ways. His presence is much more vast and magnificent than you or I have discovered to this point, and that is as it should be. How do you get to know someone? You listen to his or her heart. So it is with God.

For years I tried to know God strictly by reading His Word, the Bible. Even though I could read that Word and at times find direction for my life there, I never felt that I had direct access to God—no real relationship, in short. I finally realized that I could never have a real relationship with a book, even one as marvelous as the Bible. I had to seek the *living* Word of God, Jesus Christ (see Revelation 19:11-13). I had to establish a real, vital, heart-to-heart relationship with Him.

I grew up in a noncharismatic church, but I had a grandmother who attended the Assemblies of God church in town—a grandmother who faithfully followed the ministries of Oral Roberts, Kathryn Kuhlman, T. L. Osborn, and others of a charismatic persuasion. I can remember hearing those ministers speak of hearing the voice of God, and I would wonder why they could hear Him and I could not.

Even my grandmother told me that she often heard the Lord speak to her. She once told me that she would recognize my Grandfather Jernigan when she got to heaven because God had told her his new name in glory. I was flabbergasted, to say the least—and made more curious by such bold statements.

When I came to a point of identity crisis after college and really got desperate to know God, I began seeking to hear His voice. How did I learn? I began talking to Him in prayer with the understanding that relationship with God is a two-way street. I talk; He listens. He talks; I listen. Simple, yet revolutionary to me.

As I mentioned in the previous chapter, I began asking Him questions and waiting for answers. It is a practice I continue to this day.

And when I do that, the next thing I know, I begin to understand that He speaks with more than simple impressions upon my heart or mind. Sometimes I wake up and there's a song in my heart that I need to write down. Who put it there? Sometimes I have spiritual insights—visions, if you will—that I cannot take credit for. Who put them there? Sometimes circumstances happen that either keep me from a wrong decision or lead me to some new truth about myself or God. Who arranges these events? I have even had people who did not know me or my circumstances speak something that God had impressed upon their hearts for me—and it turned out to be nothing short of miraculous.

As you can see, God speaks in many varied and creative ways. His voice is more prevalent and magnificent than we can possibly fathom with our feeble and untrusting minds. But I must trust what He says: that He is speaking and that I can hear Him. As with any endeavor to somehow explain what we know of God, we eventually come to the point of realizing that the most we can ever do is see a tiny bit of who He is. The joy for you and me as believers is in the journey.

What a blessed adventure this life becomes when we choose to live it in relationship—in intimate communion—with our God! He has made a way for us to hear and know Him. And in hearing Him, we develop our relationship with Him and lose the fears that would keep us from being complete giant killers. Let us learn to trust that we *can* hear Him!

—

Truthstone
Joel 2:28-29
John 1:1-14
Hebrews 1:1-4

A Look Inside

1. How has God spoken to me?
2. In what ways am I more apt to hear God? (That is, in what areas am I more sensitive?)
3. How confident am I that I will be able to participate in a complete, back-and-forth conversation with God?

"Even in Their Sleep..."

Choose one of the ways in which God speaks, and ask the Holy Spirit to allow you to hear God speak in that way.

YOU ARE

Put the Enemy down underneath your feet
We are in battle and we never sound retreat
We serve the God who has assured us of our victory
Holy armor on, headed into war
Knowing who and whose we are like we've not known before
We serve the God who has assured us of our victory

You are a Giant Killer
You are the redeeming Healer
You are the One who died for me
You are the overcoming God of victory
You are the God of thunder
You are putting enemies under
You are the One who set us free
You are the overcoming God of victory

With the shield of faith, covered by the blood
We storm the gates of hell just like a mighty flood
We serve the God who has assured us of our victory
Of the risen King we will testify
We are so convinced that we are not afraid to die
We serve the God who has assured us of our victory

Overcome the lies by the blood of the Lamb
Tell what God has done for your heart and then stand
Take back the ground that the Enemy stole
Christ set you free, leaving God in control
Who is your God? Tell me who is your King

Jesus is the Lord over everything
What you gonna do when it's said and done?
Walk like a child of the Risen One?

> *I am a giant killer*
> *I am following the Healer*
> *I am His child and I'm redeemed*
> *I am an overcoming child of victory*
> *I am a son of thunder*
> *I am putting enemies under*
> *I am His child and I am free*
> *I am an overcoming child of victory*

PART

VI

THE STONE OF
PRAISE AND
WORSHIP

TWENTY-FOUR

Relationship: The Basis of Worship

W hen I had first begun to walk away from homosexuality and my mind would become filled with perverse thoughts, I had to make a decision to exchange that kind of lust for the deepest desires of my heart—to "lust" after God, so to speak. And it worked. One craving drove out another.

All of us face the Lahmi giant of evil desires in one form or another. As mentioned in chapter 9, *Lahmi* means "foodful," and he represents not just gluttony but any kind of wicked craving, including illicit sexual attraction, addiction to drugs, or whatever other desire might have us enslaved. But while Lahmi looks different in each of our lives, the stone to slay him is the same: praise and worship of God. The giant of evil desires is defeated by this stronger, purer, all-encompassing desire.

I have found that worship requires my entire being. When I worship, I use my mind, my will, my emotions, and even my body. Seeking God in this way shuts out the lies of the Enemy that try to convince me to forget about God and give in to my evil desires. There's no room for Satan in my life when my all is devoted to God.

Worship is more than I dreamed it could be when I first started learning about it. Worship is more than singing a song. More than lifting my hands. More than getting down on my knees. My expressions of worship must come from my inner relationship with God, born out of my deepest, truest identity.

Having been raised in a noncharismatic church, I had no idea there was any difference between worship and praise. Now, having had the opportunity to worship with my charismatic brothers and sisters, I realize they do not have any idea about the difference either!

Before anyone gets the wrong idea, let me affirm that I am a Spirit-filled believer. Furthermore, I desire to be a part of *the* body of Christ and not to be separated from my brothers and sisters by petty differences. Jesus Christ is Lord. Period.

I have spent the past twenty years of my life pursuing God in a way I never dreamed I would. I came to the point where I was tired of the death and dryness of my religious tradition. When I plunged into the charismatic world, I became disillusioned at the flakiness and lack of character I saw there.

What I soon realized was that I wore the grave clothes of both worlds. *Inside* I was dry and dying. *Inside* I was wishy-washy and in need of godly character—the fruit of the Spirit. Because of my recognition of my own shortcomings, I set out on a most incredible journey: to know God for myself.

I came to understand that the deepest needs of my heart would be met in one way, that the answers to all my questions would be found through one means, that I would come to know God in the deep way I desired through one thing: relationship!

In the 1996 presidential election, the Clinton campaign kept one word in the forefront of their election team's mind. "It's the *economy*, stupid," they said. By keeping their focus, they were able to fend off the distractions of the opposition and keep their heads together as a team, thereby spinning even the worst of issues to their favor by changing the subject back to the economy.

For me, *relationship* is the word God has spoken to my heart. I knew Jesus was Lord. I confessed with my mouth as much. I believed that He was the Son of God and that He had risen from the dead. I knew all the right things to say and do. I just didn't know that relationship was required, much less what it really meant.

Relationship, in its simplest form, means being connected or enjoying kinship. To me, relationship is a two-way flow. I receive the life of Christ, and I give my life back to Him. What a concept! No one had ever told me this was possible, at least not to the degree I have come to realize it in my own life.

Relationship with God is like the Sea of Galilee, while a lack of relationship is like the Dead Sea. Let me explain.

If you have seen pictures of the Sea of Galilee in northern Israel, you know what a beautiful lake it is. Green and peaceful, it receives the runoff from the surrounding hills. In turn, this lake nourishes the plant and animal life within its banks as well as the farmland of the surrounding area.

Life-giving water flows out of the Sea of Galilee, via the Jordan River, and arrives at the Dead Sea. And yet this second lake has earned its name: It is dead. Virtually nothing lives in its mineral-laden waters. Except where artificially irrigated, its shores are dry, barren, and uninhabited.

Why the difference between these two lakes? The Dead Sea is dead because even though it receives "life," it gives nothing back. Water flows into it but never flows out. In other words, the relationship between the two bodies of water is one way.

We are called to live in a two-way relationship with Jesus Christ. He is real and alive and desires an intimate and ever-deepening relationship with each one of us. After all, didn't Jesus say He would give us life and give it to us in abundance (see John 10:10)? We, for our part, return life by worshiping Him for all His greatness.

For the next few chapters, we'll look more deeply into the subject of worship (and, yes, even how worship differs from praise). Throughout it all, the message will be that we must learn to worship God through a real relationship with Him if we want to be victorious giant killers.

I've got news for you, my friend: You're going to desire something. Choose to desire God.

Truthstone
2 Chronicles 5:13-14
Psalm 51:14-17

A Look Inside
1. What sinful desires are hindering my success as a giant killer? How might establishing a lifestyle of worship help me?
2. Is my relationship with God more like the Sea of Galilee or the Dead Sea? Why?
3. What areas of my relationship with God are being hindered by the lack of a life-flow?

"Even in Their Sleep…"
Invite the Lord to break loose anything that is blocking your relationship with Him in any way.

Thank You, Lord!

In an earlier chapter, in which I described my history as a giant killer, I mentioned that my first job after college was driving a school bus—a job that gave me time to journal my thoughts every morning (see chapter 2). What I did not mention was that this job also gave me plenty of time between my morning shift and my afternoon shift. I quickly decided that God had engineered it that way to put me in a position to get to know Him.

Since I didn't even know where to begin, I simply sat at the piano bench each day between my morning route and my afternoon route and sang my heart out to the Father. At first, all I knew to do was to place my Bible on the piano, open it to the Psalms of David, and cry out David's words in song to Jesus. (That original giant killer really knew how to worship and praise God!) What I found myself doing more often than not was thanking God for all He had done in my life.

As I look back on those times, I now understand that I was taking baby steps in my journey toward knowing God. Just as a toddler learns to walk by stumbling toward the outstretched arms of his daddy, so I was stumbling in faith toward my heavenly Father. I found spiritual legs on which I no longer had to crawl but could now walk and—yes—run toward the Father. The truth is this: I had begun to praise Him through the expression of gratitude.

Indeed, as I sang through the Psalms day after day, I discovered that whenever David used words of praise, they were almost always explicitly in a context of gratitude. A remarkable king, songwriter, and slingsman, David extolled the ways in which God had benefited his life. Other psalmists echo David's attitude. In Psalm 107, the psalmist praises God and calls us to join him:

> Give thanks to the LORD, for he is good;
>   his love endures forever.
> Let the redeemed of the LORD say this—
>   those he redeemed from the hand of the foe. (verses 1-2)

From the examples of the psalm writers, I discovered that praise is giving thanks to God for who He is and for what He has done.

Having been set free from the sin of homosexuality in 1981, I had gratitude toward God on my mind. I felt an affinity with Paul, the "chief of all sinners," who said, "I thank Christ Jesus our Lord, who has given me strength, that he considered me faithful, appointing me to his service. Even though I was once a blasphemer and a persecutor and a violent man, I was shown mercy because I acted in ignorance and unbelief" (1 Timothy 1:12-13; see also verse 15). I could replace "a blasphemer and a persecutor and a violent man" in that statement with "a homosexual and a hypocrite and a prideful man," and the words would fit me perfectly. How amazing was God's mercy toward me! I had to tell Him how I felt. It marked a revolution in my life.

So this is how it works: Gratitude expressed becomes praise. Praise becomes a springboard into the deeper places of relationship with almighty God. Relationship with God fills our hearts and precludes relationship with any evil giant.

As you are in the midst of fighting a giant, you may be more focused on what is wrong in your life than on what is right with it. But if you will try, I am certain that you will be able to remember much that God has done for you in the past and even identify much that He is doing for you right now. Go to God and tell Him how grateful you are for His kindness toward you. If you are bold enough, praise Him *in advance* for how He is going to give you final victory over your giant.

Your praise can take any form that's natural for you. Sing it, like me and like David, if you want to. Or tell God in prayer how you feel about Him. Be as creative or as straightforward with your praise as you like. Just make sure that you are honestly expressing your sense of gratitude to Him.

And now I have a caution for you.

I believe that gratitude should be the attitude of every worshiper, yet the truth is that even a nonbeliever can express gratitude to God for something He has done. One can believe in God (in some sense, anyway) and yet not know Him. In other words, praise does not necessarily require relationship with God.

I have seen people, devoid of a life-changing relationship with God, receive something (like healing or financial gain) and readily thank God for what He had done, only to go right back to the ungodly lives they had lived prior to God's intervention. I would be willing to bet that you have known people who do just the same.

Certainly we have all seen movies in which the hero is lost at sea or finds himself in some dire situation. At some point he makes a statement like "God, if You get me out of this, I'll change my ways." Of course, the hero always makes it, and he thanks God verbally, but apparently nothing else in his life changes. Did he praise God? Yes. Did he have a relationship with Him? I would say he did not.

It's the same in real life: One can praise God and not know Him. But I believe one cannot *worship* God without a true knowledge of Him—that is, without a "knowing" relationship, an intimate spiritual connection. Make sure, then, that you are both a praiser and a worshiper. Offer thanks to God from out of the depths of your relationship with Him.

You may not be a bus driver with plenty of free time on your hands, as I was in 1981. You may not be able to turn psalms into songs at a piano. Nevertheless, you can begin taking baby steps toward the welcoming arms of your Father—He will make a way for you. Cry out to Him in whatever way you can. Tell Him how thankful you are for every victory He has sent and will continue to send you.

What does Lahmi, giant of evil desires, look like in your life? How fearsome does he appear to you? Whatever your case may be, know that you can send old Lahmi slinking away over the hills if you will fill your life with the praise of God's goodness.

Truthstone
Psalm 30
Luke 17:11-19
Colossians 3:15-17

A Look Inside
1. What is the role of gratitude in my relationship with God? in my identity as a giant killer?
2. How can I live my life as praise to God?

"Even in Their Sleep…"
Spend some time before bed thinking about all that is good in your life. Then thank God in detail for all of it—especially for His gracious nature.

Knowing and Known

I used to think God was a cosmic policeman who showed an inter-
est in me only when I messed up. When I sinned He would zoom
into my life, zap me with some punishment, then zoom out again to
resume His distant and controlling stance over me (much like the
"church police," our modern-day Pharisees). Or so I thought.

What I have since come to see is that God is not distant at all but
is as near to me as I will allow Him to be. Not only that, but He also
speaks to me as I speak to Him.

I sing to Him; He sings to me.

I dance before Him; He dances with me.

I bow; He cleanses me.

I fall; He picks me up.

I seek to know who I am; He gives me my identity.

Do you get the picture? There is way more to God than we have
ever realized—or ever will.

Far from wanting to zap me for my sins, God wants to show me
His love. He wants to draw near to me as I draw near to Him. But
how does one get to know the Creator of the universe in such an intimate way? The way I live out my relationship with the Father is
through worship.

Our word *worship* is a shortened form of an older English word
worthship. Literally, then, to worship is to acknowledge the worth of

something. The "living creatures" of Revelation 4 were truly worshiping when they said to God, "You are worthy, our Lord and God, to receive glory and honor and power" (verse 11).

We worship as we recognize the greatness of God.

But "to acknowledge God's worthship" is a very general definition of worship. It takes us only so far. More specifically, I would suggest this definition: We worship by living out our relationship with God through Jesus Christ by the power of the Holy Spirit.

Proverbs 3:5-6 is one of those Bible passages that are perennial favorites to memorize, and for a good reason. These verses say:

> Trust in the LORD with all your heart
>   and lean not on your own understanding;
> in all your ways acknowledge him,
>   and he will make your paths straight.

In other words, if I will seek to *know* God in, with, and through every aspect of my life, He will direct my paths. He wants to be intimately involved in my life. And as I open up to that kind of relationship, I am worshiping.

So, let's consider this: If worship is living out our relationship with Father, what do we do, exactly? In the simplest terms, worship is obedience to God. Obedience requires surrender of our wills to God's will. It means admitting that He knows best how we should live.

Giving up our wills, in this sense, does not involve a loss of personal identity, as we see in many cults. Rather, my obedience and my subsequent surrender mean I understand that I desperately need God—I need Him even more than I need the air I breathe.

Who made the air I breathe? Who gave me life in the first place? Who overcame my homosexuality (which I could not overcome myself—I tried!) and bore it on the cross for me? I could do none of these things for myself. I certainly could not save myself. Only One could do that for me: Jesus Christ. The truth is that I need Him to meet every need of my life, and, ultimately, He does.

Do you know God to the depths that you desire? Do you think you know all you need to know of Him?

I admit, there are days when I find it difficult to hear God and to know Him in an intimate way. But isn't the recognition and confession of that need the first step in a relationship? At least I'm struggling to get closer to God.

The apostle Paul faced the same reality when he wrote to the church in Corinth. He confessed that he did not know God as fully as he desired. And he even confessed that he could see God only dimly at times: "Now we see but a poor reflection as in a mirror; then we shall see face to face. Now I know in part; then I shall know fully, even as I am fully known" (1 Corinthians 13:12).

Worship is presenting our hearts to God and saying, "Lord, here I am. I cannot see You, for the dust of this life has settled on the glass of my heart, obscuring my view. Would You please take me to Yourself and wipe off that dust so I might see You and know You better?"

Worship, then, is communion or back-and-forth communication with God. God sees us—even the things we hide—and He still loves us. God desires that we have an honest and open relationship with Him. But to know God is to realize that we cannot know Him without being changed. Change is good because God's change brings us closer to the reality of who we really were created to be: more like Him, our Father.

As with healing, honesty requires confession. Confession requires trust. Trust paves the way for relationship. Relationship is the conduit—the vessel—of life. God just wants us to be honest.

God seeks to know those who will worship Him in spirit and in truth, as we learn in John 4:23-24. The simplest interpretation of this scripture is that whatever I express on the outside (the truth) should flow from what is on the inside (the spirit). People will hear my words, but they will look at my life to see if there really is power or life in what I say.

God Himself looks at the heart rather than at the outer person (see 1 Samuel 16:7). Shouldn't that tell us something about what it means to be a worshiper? Let's be like the apostle Paul, who declared,

> We refuse to wear masks and play games. We don't maneuver and manipulate behind the scenes. And we don't twist God's Word to suit ourselves. Rather, we keep everything we do and say out in the open, the whole truth on display, so that those who want to can see and judge for themselves in the presence of God. (2 Corinthians 4:2, MSG)

God desires that we be either hot or cold (see Revelation 3:15). This is simply another aspect of transparency or honesty with God. A worshiper must worship out of love for the Father and out of genuine love for those he or she leads or desires to reach. Otherwise, that love is just so much noise (see 1 Corinthians 13).

These days I understand that God is no cosmic policeman, and I'm not afraid of His zapping me anymore. But even without the motive of fear (or rather, *because* I have no fear), I want to obey Him and live for Him. I'll be honest with Him about my confusion and my shortcomings, and I'll keep searching for Him until I can see Him face to face.

Truthstone
Micah 6:6-8
John 4:19-24
Revelation 7:9-12

A Look Inside
1. How much am I worth to God? How much is He worth to me?
2. How can I live out my relationship with God more fully through obedience?
3. How can I express the communion I enjoy with God?

"Even in Their Sleep..."
In prayer this evening, acknowledge the worth you place upon the Lord because of who He is in your life.

Freely Worship

T he beauty of any relationship that is filled with life and bears fruit is that it is entered into by choice. As it is in human relationships, so it is in our relationship with God. He does not force us to love Him. Rather, He freely chose us, and He allows us freedom to choose Him in return.

So why do we find verses in the Bible that command us to love and worship Him? To take only one example, He commanded, "Love the LORD your God with all your heart and with all your soul and with all your strength" (Deuteronomy 6:5). Why such a command?

I believe it is because God provided the Law to be like a teacher that guides us to the truth. Ultimately, we need God and we need to know Him. Like a teacher who assigns homework because she knows that her students will need that knowledge in their later lives, the Father blessed us with His Law because He knew we would need to know Him if we are to succeed at life.

The Law serves an important purpose in that it shows us our need for a Savior. Yet we must remember that although God commands us to worship, He still gives us free choice. He will never force us to worship Him in this life.

The Bible gives us a glimpse of a time (after Christ's return) when some may be forced to worship Christ.

At the name of Jesus every knee [will] bow,
in heaven and on earth and under the earth,
and every tongue confess that Jesus Christ is Lord,
to the glory of God the Father. (Philippians 2:10-11)

If those who are "under the earth" are people in hell—people who have chosen Satan instead of God—then presumably they will confess Jesus Christ under duress.

That future time of forced worship only makes it more remarkable to think that *right now* God gives us the freedom to choose to worship Him or not. He loves us so much that He wants us to worship Him by choice. That's a better situation by far—for us and for Him.

Who would want to feel that the love he received had been forced out of others? That would not be love; that would be slavery, devoid of relationship. God knows this, and because he values relationship, He allows us the dangerous choice of worshiping Him or not.

Remember, He is a God of risk who is willing to give us the opportunity to love Him of our own accord. I know I love it when my children express their love to me without coercion from me. God must feel the same way toward us, His children.

In one sense, of course, there really isn't a decision to make. Without a doubt, we should *want* to worship God. Our understanding of who He is, however flawed that understanding may be, should be enough to move us to worship Him for His wonderful love, power, mercy, goodness, and holiness. Our understanding of our own indebtedness to Him, as His creatures who have sinned against Him and have been forgiven, should likewise move us to worship.

God is the Creator; we are the creation. The creation reflects the heart of the One who created it. If He loved us, then isn't it our hearts' deepest desire to love Him? Isn't it the heart cry of all humankind to know God? I believe that if we were honest, we would have to say that there is an emptiness—a void—deep inside that compels us to know our purpose for existence. For the believer in Christ, that purpose is more easily seen.

Again, we see why the Law is needed: to guide unbelievers to see their need for something to fill that void, for something greater than themselves. All that God created was created to bring Him glory—to reveal the createdness that is who we are. The only way to fully know and live in that reality is to come to grips with a relationship with the Creator of all that is.

> You are worthy, our Lord and God,
> > to receive glory and honor and power,
> *for you created all things,*
> > *and by your will they were created*
> > *and have their being.* (Revelation 4:11, emphasis added)

Worship puts us in our proper position in relation to God. It is an admission that He is the perfect God and we are his creation. Worship, then, can be considered an act of confession in which we agree with God that we need Him.

The wonderful thing about confession is that it brings healing. James 5:16 says, "Confess your sins to each other and pray for each other so that you may be healed. The prayer of a righteous man is powerful and effective." As we confess our sins to each other and especially to God, the sickness of our souls begins to heal.

How does confession bring healing? To answer that, let me ask another question. If I went to a physician seeking healing for a certain ailment but would not tell him where I hurt, how could I be healed? Confession identifies our soul sickness and lets the treatment begin.

Confession is not for the doctor but for the patient. Yes, God knows where we hurt, but do we trust God—the Great Physician—enough to allow ourselves to be vulnerable with Him? Being honest about our condition is an essential part of our healing.

Sin is the ultimate ailment. When the "cells" of our hearts have been rid of the "bacteria" of sin by the "antibiotics" of Christ's redeeming blood, life is no longer hampered, and the flow of relationship is once again restored. Healing of the soul takes place.

On countless occasions while leading worship, I have asked others to get honest about their need for God in some area of their lives. During one particular New Year's Eve service, I felt compelled to ask if there was anyone in the audience who was contemplating suicide. Expecting one or two to stand for ministry, I was overwhelmed when more than forty people stood!

What has that got to do with worship? I believe that in the atmosphere of worship, God's love wooed those hurting hearts to get honest about their needs and to express those needs as an act of love and trust—an act of worship. Worship brought them the chance of healing.

If we desire health in our souls, we must feed our souls with the proper diet: a diet of relationship with God through the food of praise and worship.

> How good it is to sing praises to our God,
>   how pleasant and fitting to praise him! (Psalm 147:1)

In other words, praise looks good on you. Praise does a body and soul good. If praise does that, then worship—the depth of relationship—will do the same...and more!

God does not coerce you into worshiping Him. But don't you want to do it anyway? For one battered and bruised by a giant, nothing will bring healing and a return of strength quite like a dose of worship.

Truthstone
Psalm 63:1-8
Psalm 95:6-7
Hebrews 13:15

A Look Inside
1. Do I worship God out of a sense of duty or because I really want to? Why?
2. What reasons do I have to worship God?
3. How could worship help to bring me the spiritual healing I need?

"Even in Their Sleep…"
Tonight, spend time meditating on who God is and what He has done for you. Then, in the freedom the Holy Spirit gives, pour out your worship to God.

We Win

Don't give up, don't give in
When you fall, get right back up again
And lift your eyes toward the finish
And the One to whom you race
Run with all your might
Into the waiting, open arms of your Redeemer's embrace

> *He will level every mountain*
> *He will calm the raging sea*
> *He will comfort you in sorrow*
> *Lead you to your destiny*
> *He will pour grace out upon you*
> *Walk with you intimately*
> *He will cheer for you every step*
> *Along the way to victory*
> *So don't give up, don't give in*

Don't give up, don't give in
When you feel alone, cry out to Him
For He will never, ever leave you
Always near, His love and grace
Lift your arms up in surrender
To the waiting, open arms of your Redeemer's embrace

> *He will bear your heavy burdens*
> *Hold your head up when you're weak*
> *He will fight for you in battle*
> *Lead you when you cannot see*

He will delight in you with singing
Meet you in your greatest need
Patiently He waits for you
To trust Him with who you will be
So don't give up, don't give in
Take a look at the end of the book
And you'll find out there is no doubt we win

We win, for the work upon the cross has set us free
We win because the blood has cleansed our hearts, left us redeemed
We win and now the enemy is underneath our feet
We win because we follow Jesus Christ the risen King

He will bind your broken heart up
Tear down walls and set you free
He will carry you when weary
Hold you when you're cold and weak
He will conquer every giant
Every foe will bow the knee
At the precious name of Jesus
His shed blood our victory
So don't give up, don't give in
Take a look at the end of the book
And you'll find out there is no doubt we win

PART

VII

THE STONE OF
DREAMS FOR
THE FUTURE

Visions and Dreams

When I began my journey through healing and deliverance—
overcoming homosexuality, anger, and other spiritual problems—more than twenty years ago, little did I know the twists and turns that journey would entail. But my, what a ride it has been!

One of the most important things I have discovered (and somehow I understood this early on) is the value of knowing where I want to go. Sounds simple, but many people have no idea where they want to wind up. I'm thankful that God revealed to me the danger of aimlessness and the benefit of living with a sense of direction and purpose.

Do you know where you are going in life? Do you know where you are going spiritually?

If you're in the middle of fighting a giant in your life, you may be hoping for nothing more than to survive the next day or week. I can sympathize. I know that the giant Six Fingers, or the false sense of enslavement to sin, can seem to be unshakable, however hard we try to slip away from him (see chapter 10). Nevertheless, I encourage you to look beyond your current problems toward the place of spiritual health and achievement to which God is leading you.

In faith, trust that you can move past the sin or other spiritual problem in your life. Believe that you can do more than survive; you can thrive. You can accomplish great things for God in the years remaining to you on this earth. Striving for those objectives is part of successfully defeating old Six Fingers.

Long centuries ago a man of God named Joel prophesied that one day people endowed with the Holy Spirit would "dream dreams" and "see visions" (Joel 2:28). My Christian friend, that's us! We have the Holy Spirit, and if we will open our minds to God, He will plant individual dreams and visions in our minds. These dreams and visions have the power to make us the men and women God always meant for us to be.

The vision, the dream—that's where we are headed.

If I want to learn a new skill, such as guitar playing, I set goals for myself. If I want to improve my relationship with my kids, I set goals for how I want to spend time with them and interact with them. The same principle I apply to my everyday life is one I have applied to my spiritual identity: I have to have a target to shoot for.

When the Lord set me free from the sin of homosexuality, I immediately began to set goals for myself in a spiritual sense. I determined that I would never get anywhere if I did not know where I wanted to go. And for me, the end of the journey was knowing Jesus intimately and being set free from all my past failures. Along the way I wanted to lead others to that same freedom.

Well, since I wanted to be free, I headed for freedom. I did not know what my first step should look like, so I just did what I knew to do and headed toward Jesus. After all, no journey can begin unless the first step is taken, and I can't think of a better direction to step than toward Jesus Christ.

As I got better at this pursuing-a-spiritual-goal thing, I learned to ask myself some key questions. One of the first questions I asked myself was this: "When I get to the end of life, what would I like to have accomplished?" If I didn't ponder the answer to this question, I could easily have filled up my time with second- and third-rate uses of my energies, and so the years would dribble away. At the end of it all, I would taste the bitterness of regret.

Another question that helped me was this: "Will I stand before my

Father and rejoice that I stepped out in faith, or will I stand in shame knowing I didn't even try?" I decided I would try. I am weak in myself, but in Christ I am strong. I believed then, and I believe now, that God honors those who boldly seek to fulfill His will for their lives. Better to try and fail, and then try again (and perhaps fail again), than never to try at all.

The next question I asked to help me define my journey's final destination was this: "What are the limitations that could keep me from fulfilling my dreams?" I could think of many possible limitations. Yet as I set out on the journey toward freedom, I decided that God, rather than the obstacles that stood in my way, would be the determining factor in what I achieved.

Would I allow a lack of money to keep me from my goals? Certainly not. A lack of money does not decide my fate. I trust God, the Great Provider, to make a way where there seems to be no way.

Would I allow a lack of time to determine my final destination? No way! If there doesn't seem to be enough time to go around, then maybe I need to allow the Father to help me reprioritize my efforts.

What about my age? When I was younger, I decided I would not limit myself because others did not consider me mature enough. I would follow God and let my life be a demonstration of the depth of my experience with God. More recently, I have decided that old age will not determine or limit my dreams. I will never be too old to learn or too old to serve God.

Will I allow a lack of abilities to keep me from realizing my dreams? If I have a vision or a dream from the Lord, then I should make the necessary sacrifices to acquire whatever ability I need to fulfill that dream (like taking up the guitar in my forties!).

Will I allow the expectations of others to keep me from my dreams? If I had listened to the voices from my old life, I would have given up in defeat. If I had listened to the self-commissioned church police, I would never have ministered in a public way at all.

What else? Fear of man? Man did not die for my sins or set me free. Fear of failure? The greatest successes in life are born of failures along the way. Location? I'll go wherever the Father sends me. Resources? My God is the Maker of it all.

The bottom line? We limit ourselves by not dreaming big as our Father does. We must learn to see obstacles to our dreams and visions the way we view the giants in our lives—like one more bump along the road that gives us the opportunity to tap into the creativity of our God.

Truthstone
John 14:12-14
2 Corinthians 4:7-18
Philippians 3:12-14

A Look Inside
1. What are my visions and dreams?
2. What are the obstacles that could stand in the way of the fulfillment of my dreams?
3. When I get to the end of life, what would I like to have accomplished?

"Even in Their Sleep…"
Meditate on what you would like your life to look like when you are seventy years old. Then talk to God about how to get there.

TWENTY-NINE

A Runner Who Runs

Some years ago my friend J. Daniel Smith began running. As I observed what his new exercise regimen did for him, I saw that he dropped forty pounds in a year. He felt better. He looked great. His overall attitude was positive. Running transformed my friend.

I saw what running did for Dan, and I wanted the same benefits for myself. What if I had purchased an expensive pair of running shoes, bought some comfortable exercise clothes, and gotten up early in the morning to stretch and limber up—and then gone directly back to bed? It would hardly have done me much good, would it?

If I wanted the benefits of running, I had to actually run. And I did. I followed Dan's example and began running every day. In fact, running became an important and beneficial part of my life (or at least it was until my Achilles tendon rupture put an end to it, temporarily).

Did you know that you are a runner, in a spiritual sense? One biblical writer exhorted, "Let us run with perseverance the race marked out for us" (Hebrews 12:1). A runner in an actual footrace is instructed to keep his or her eyes fixed on the finish line. What is our finish line? "Let us fix our eyes on Jesus, the author and perfecter of our faith" (verse 2).

If life is a race and Jesus is the goal, how does one prepare for that race?

A world-class runner does not suddenly become world class without lots of road time. I believe the best runners are those who see running as their calling in life. The best runners are the ones who set goals for themselves and then head for those goals no matter how far or difficult they may seem. Most of all, the best runners are those who don't simply dream about or talk about running; the best runners are those who actually put feet to the pavement and run.

A runner must decide that she is a runner. When people know who they are, they tend to operate in confidence concerning where they are headed and what they are to do to get there. If I am called to be an overcomer, then my name—my calling—helps me determine where I am going and what I will do. In other words, I will overcome any obstacle that keeps me from Jesus, and I will do it by being who I am in relationship with Jesus.

A runner must know what type of race she is running. A sprinter will train differently than a long-distance runner. A sprinter must build up her body for short bursts of speed, while those who compete in marathons must be able to run for long periods of time. In the race of life, we are called to run for distance. There may be times when short bursts of speed are required, but for the most part, we are called to run the distance.

A runner must also know her strengths and weaknesses and train accordingly. In my own life, I know I give in to emotion rather easily. Emotional responses can be a weakness, but God has called me to turn my weakness into a strength. How? By learning my Father's emotions and asking Him to let me feel what He feels and respond as He would respond to life's trying situations.

I am a naturally tenacious person. One of my personal strengths has been an attitude that says, "Don't tell me I can't do something. I will do exactly what you say I can't do just to show you I can!" (Hmm, maybe that *is* a weakness.) When I am down and the Enemy tries to capitalize on my depression, my tenacity shifts into gear, and I fight with every bit of strength I have and capitalize upon that strength.

My point is this: I allow the Coach to reveal to me both my weaknesses and my strengths and then to lead me through the proper use of both.

To strengthen my spiritual legs, I must practice the truth while running the short "legs" of the race. For example, when the car gets a flat and I am in a hurry, I may be tempted to lash out at my wife and children. But my Trainer urges me to put on patience and endure the trial, thus building up my muscles little by little. Daily practice of "running" builds up my endurance, for the day will come when I will be attacked by those opposed to my stand for righteousness, and I will respond with endurance rather than being overwhelmed—because I trained each and every day.

A runner must run. That may sound funny because it is one of those "duh" statements. Yet how many people have you met who talk about enduring the race of life but in actuality seem to be victims who never overcome or win? Instead, they are overcome by their circumstances and are always on the losing side simply because they do not get up and run.

If I had waited to write a book until everyone believed I could write one, I would never have written a book. While I had a vision for putting my heart into writing several years ago, I did not wait for a publisher to approach me. I wrote what was in my heart. And in so doing, I began to learn how to write.

By actually running the race of writing a book, I learned how to endure the hours, weeks, and months required to see that book come to pass. In other words, I did not talk and dream of writing a book; I actually wrote a book. And guess what? When I was approached by a publisher, I had already built up the stamina and had already trained for that day. I called upon what I had trained for and ran the race. I won because I had gotten up and done what I envisioned, because I knew this is who I am.

Yes, I fall many times in life's race. But I do not allow the Enemy to use such stumbles to cause me to give up or alter my course.

Rather, I use the Enemy's taunts to empower me to get up and keep running. Micah 7:8 says, "Do not gloat over me, my enemy! Though I have fallen, I will rise."

What this means to me is this: I do not plan to fall, but I do have a plan for the times when I may fall. I will rise and turn back toward Jesus no matter what, and I will run toward Him with all my might.

Believer, we are called to know Christ in an intimate way in this life. The Enemy knows this and hates it, and he will try to keep it from happening. As a runner, you must get up and run in spite of any possible excuses. I urge you to be who you are and to run with all your might toward the goal. Run the race by running the race! And trust Jesus to be there with you every step of the way.

Truthstone
1 Corinthians 9:24-27
Philippians 2:14-16
2 Timothy 4:6-8
Hebrews 12:1-4

A Look Inside
1. Am I running the race God has laid out before me? If not, why not?
2. How can I build up endurance?
3. How can I keep running when my strength is gone or my hopes have been shattered?

"Even in Their Sleep…"
Ask the Lord to show you His training regimen for your life. Rest in knowing that He is with You every step of the way.

THIRTY

The Goals of My Life

When I set out on my journey toward knowing Christ, I determined what my dreams and visions were. I envisioned myself free from homosexuality (that giant defeated) and free from bitterness toward those who had hurt me, and I began to set goals to help me get to that ultimate destination. If I had set out with the delusional idea that I would get there instantly, I would have given up a long time ago. Healing is a journey, and any successful journey is really progress toward a series of goals established beforehand.

What, exactly, is a goal? According to Dorothy Lemkuhl, author of *Organizing for the Creative Person,* a goal is "a dream set within a time frame." I wish I had thought of that definition. It captures my idea of my relationship with Christ and my journey toward freedom.

With the help of the Holy Spirit, I had a dream for freedom from bondage, and I began to set that dream, or goal, into a time frame. What was my time frame? Well, I didn't have specific dates in mind. I just wanted to see my goals accomplished in God's time. The point for me was to begin the journey, and God would help me set the time frame along the way. My first goal was to get started, and my first target time was immediately!

Where did I begin? I began where I would end: with God. I knew I needed His Word, His Spirit, and His mind to get me where I wanted to go.

I began early in my journey toward freedom to hide God's Word in my heart. I memorized verses I thought would be helpful to me. Then, whenever a temptation would come or an obstacle would rise up, I would remind myself of the truth by remembering what God's Word had to say on the subject. In this way, I knew I was headed in the right direction, and I remembered that God's Word was always right on time.

Along with God's Word, I had the presence of the Holy Spirit to help me determine the steps and timing along the way. Scripture tells us that God's Spirit comes alongside us to guide us, and if we will keep in step with Him, we will never go astray (see Galatians 5:25). Most of all, knowing I have the Spirit reminds me that I am never alone.

I also began to learn that if God had truly made me a new creation, then I had His mind (see 1 Corinthians 2:16). He will reveal truths to me, as a Christian, that unspiritual people could never comprehend. These truths may include basic facts about who He is, and they may also include specific directions for what He wants to do in my life. He has graciously granted me access to these important thoughts.

Having God's Word, God's Spirit, and God's mind has meant so much in my journey. They have helped me set and reach one goal after another. May I share with you a few tips I've learned over the years about setting goals?

I've learned that one of the most vital points in setting goals is to recognize that I have them. Due to fear of failure or fear of what others might think, I might be tempted to hide my visions and dreams. But I will never accomplish anything if I never admit I have a vision. I must get honest with myself, honest with the Lord, and honest with others. I have to remember Jesus's words: "You will know [have a personal encounter with] the truth, and the truth will set you free" (John 8:32).

I have also discovered the value of being careful about whom I share my visions and dreams with. I avoid sharing them with those who might seek to manipulate me or with those who might be negative about my goals or my abilities. I see my dreams as precious pearls.

I would never spread those pearls before swine (see Matthew 7:6). Pigs don't understand the value of pearls, and while rooting around, they would trample on those pearls.

I would rather share my pearls with those who will help me polish them and present them to the Lord in the best possible condition. So I share my dreams with those who will not trample them, because I determined early on that I would obey God rather than men.

In addition, I have learned to be deliberate and orderly about how I set my goals. Once a year I sit down and determine my goals. Of course, I know I will need to revise and add to my goals in the course of the year. But setting aside a specific time to focus on my goals is helpful to me.

I first seek God to determine what His vision for my life is, then I build my visions and dreams around that, both verbalizing my goals to others and writing them down. As I seek God, I try to focus on His heart because I desire for His heart to be communicated through the unique vessel He created me to be, and I simply try to stay true to my heart (who He called me to be) once I have discerned His heart. I basically try to set goals according to God's plan for my life.

I love to give myself a timetable when setting my goals. I believe it is important that we set for ourselves small, achievable goals that lead up to the big goals of our lives. In this way, we are able to see progress and we gain encouragement along the way. By putting goals on the calendar, I effectively give myself a finish line to run for—or a little giant to put down, if you will.

I also tell others—my wife and close friends—what my goals are, allowing them the freedom to ask me about them from time to time. More often than not, I do not wait for them to ask me about my goals and my progress toward meeting them. I give them updates frequently and ask them to pray for me and hold me accountable. Because I know others are there to help me, I am greatly motivated to put off the old and put on the new.

Along the way, I have found it important to surround myself with wise men and women who will help me seek Jesus as I seek to establish goals for my life.

Plans fail for lack of counsel,
>   but with many advisers they succeed. (Proverbs 15:22)

I am thankful to God for giving me so many wise and caring friends. God will give you friends like that too, if you ask Him.

To do all of these things as a goal setter, I must humble myself, which means I must avoid pride. God is God; I am not. The goal of goal setting is not to bring glory and honor to myself but to bring glory and honor to the only One worthy: our wonderful Lord God.

Truthstone
Psalm 37:4
Proverbs 4:25-27
Isaiah 54:2-3

A Look Inside
1. What goals must I set to see my dreams come to pass?
2. What time frames will I set for my goals?
3. What and who can help me achieve my goals?

"Even in Their Sleep…"
Ask God to allow you to see yourself on the journey toward the completion of a spiritual goal in your life.

THIRTY-ONE

Limits and Priorities

"All things are possible with God," said Jesus in Mark 10:27. And
I believe Him. If God wants us to accomplish something, and
if He is all-powerful (as surely He is), then how could we fail to do
the "impossible" with Him assisting us? That's why I set bold goals for
myself and encourage others to do the same. But along the way, I have
learned to live in the reality of my circumstances when setbacks have
occurred.

Hear me now: Living in the reality of circumstances does not
equal living in defeat. Setbacks and limitations may change our timetable for achieving our goals. They may even force us to redefine our
goals or redirect our paths. But they don't prevent us from achieving
God's goals for us (maybe our original goals weren't the right ones). I
have thus learned, by painful experience, to interpret setbacks and
limitations as opportunities for creativity.

Let me illustrate how it works.

I like to play basketball, and I like to think that I'm pretty good
at it. One day in March 2001, during a basketball game with friends,
I suddenly felt a terrible ripping pain on the back side of my left leg.
Diagnosis? Severed Achilles tendon.

If you've ever had this injury (and for your sake, I hope you have
not), you know that it is extremely painful. It also takes a long time
to heal. After undergoing surgery to reattach my tendon, I was told to
expect months of rehabilitation, during which I would not be able to

use my leg as I was used to. No basketball. No running. No walking, even, for a while. I would be doing a lot of sitting—in chairs and wheelchairs.

At first I wanted to give up. I was discouraged. No, I was beyond discouraged. But rather than wallow in self-pity or sit around doing nothing for weeks, I set several goals for myself. In this way, I gave myself some hope that things would not always be this way, even if I remained crippled for life.

Would you like to know the goals I set for myself that year? Here they are:

1. I will practice my guitar while I sit here for the next few weeks.
2. I will continue to travel and minister.
3. I will learn to humble myself and ask for help.
4. I will work hard at physical therapy and be playing basketball again by the one-year anniversary of my injury.
5. I will ski next season.

How many of those goals did I meet? I now play the guitar during ministry times—in public. I continued to minister both before and after my surgery. Because I had to ask for help, I arrived at a new level of humility, and I gained a new level of intimacy with those I trusted to carry me or push me around. And weeks ahead of the one-year anniversary of my injury, I was already playing basketball with my children, and I had skied three times.

Though I had to give up many things in the process of healing, other things rose to the surface of my life. These new emphases and activities in my life have been the fruit of God's vision for me as His child. When circumstances blocked my way, God's creativity made another way. That's what He does. My part is trusting in Him.

During my recovery from the Achilles tendon injury, I maintained intimacy with God because I knew I needed Him. As I relied on God, my levels of patience and hope remained high, even when I was physically immobilized and in intense pain. I believe that when times like these occur, it is vital to remember to prioritize our lives (our visions, dreams, goals) according to what God calls important.

How did my goals for recovery line up with God's? When I felt I had a handle on the answer to that question, I could do away with all the things that cried for my attention but did not meet the priority status. I still wanted to help around the farm, but I had to rely on others to get the work done. I had to give up going to the movies with my buddies for a while, but I learned to spend the evenings with my children, singing as a family. I had to run the new race set before me and realize that the altered course would still get me where I was going. I had to learn to not be afraid to let things go undone, especially if they did not serve God's purpose or were more of a distraction than a benefit.

During my recovery I learned that urgent does not always equal important. There were so many more things that needed my attention than the items on the to-do lists of my life. I, in effect, was learning to spend my life wisely.

God sets the agenda for my life. When I submit to that reality—that is, when I let Him be God and me be His child—I realize that physical limits mean nothing to Him. What may appear as major limits to my life and plans are, in fact, catalysts to greater creativity and deeper levels of intimacy with God.

A setback or even a failure is not a reason to quit. I see both as springboards to deeper places in God's creative heart. Even while on crutches for months, I determined that I would see each of my goals through—one way or another—until I heard otherwise from God. To not complete a task lends weight to the lies of the Enemy, and his lies always lead away from God's best right down to the pit of discouragement and ultimate defeat.

That's not where I'm headed. God has me on an upward course, despite temporary setbacks. I am a giant killer!

—

Truthstone
Proverbs 19:21
Matthew 6:25-34
Luke 9:59-62

A Look Inside
1. What circumstances, if any, have made me feel like giving up lately?
2. What is God's vision for my life as His child?
3. How could my limitations serve as springboards to greater levels of God's creativity in and through me?

"Even in Their Sleep…"
Give the Holy Spirit freedom to lead you around, over, or through your limitations and fill you with a clearer vision of God's creative power in your life.

When Dreams Fall Apart

As I received the vision to record an album called *Giant Killer*, I assumed it would be the next one in line for me. Through a series of circumstances, though, this recording had to be put on hold so I could record an album called *I Surrender*. (Appropriate name, huh?) This would turn out to be the first of many delays.

When I was finally released to begin recording *Giant Killer*, I felt I was to produce it myself. So my friend Tim and I began the process of recording. Everything went smoothly up until the day we were scheduled to record the live portion of the project.

I felt lightheaded on the day of the event. By the time I got to the recording venue, I could hardly maintain my balance. I felt miserable. I didn't even get to enjoy the catered barbecue beforehand, much less the actual worship time.

As we concluded the evening, I asked if there was a doctor in the house (I have always wanted to say that!). There was none. Too weak even to greet the hundreds of people who had graciously come to take part in the recording, I had to go lie down. The diagnosis? Sinus infection coupled with an inner-ear infection.

I got treatment for the infections, but they were stubborn. As the day for mixing approached, it became evident that I was still too ill to make the plane ride to Nashville for the mix. That meant I would be in violation of my recording contract, since the master mix of the recording was (by contract) to be delivered by the end of November.

My record label graciously gave me an extension, but I had to wait until January of the next year to finally get to Nashville for the mix. And guess what? As soon as I got there and the mixing began, the inner-ear infection recurred. I came home without the master mix being completed.

Not only had I missed the first deadline; I had missed the extension as well. I felt like giving up. Almost three years had passed since the time I had received the songs and the vision for the project. Talk about being patient or weary—I fell more on the weary side of things! What to do?

I had to get back to the truth, of course. The truth is what God calls the truth, even when the world says otherwise. Either I could give in, as the Enemy desired, or I could keep my eyes on Jesus and carry out the task before me. As I committed to the latter course, my attitude changed. My body began to heal, and I made it back to Nashville for the final mix. Hard work? Yes! Long haul? Duh! Victorious? You betcha!

Recording mixed, God glorified, vision accomplished.

All of us will face times in our lives when the plans and hopes and dreams we have held for ourselves or others unravel. Sometimes death puts an end to a friendship we always thought would be there. Sometimes people grow apart or move away. Sometimes bad stuff just happens. If a vision is from God, though, nothing can keep it from fulfillment. The fulfillment just may not be what we had perceived with our fallible human minds.

When obstacles block my way, I choose to believe God rather than my circumstances, and I do what I can. Like the ant preparing for the winter it knows is coming (see Proverbs 6:6-8), I work toward my goals even when it does not seem necessary, because I want to be ready when the time for completion is at hand. I try to live for today but know who holds the future. Like the virgins in Matthew 25:1-13, I must prepare wisely because I never know when the Lord will call for me to come and complete the goal. I believe that the devil has a scheme but that God has a plan, so I plan to keep running the race even when I fall along the way.

Above all, I see Christ as the ultimate goal I am trying to achieve. I seek Him in faith along the way (see Hebrews 11:6). I want to know Him because to know Him is fulfillment and satisfaction like nothing else (see Philippians 3:8-11).

The journey is where joy and anticipation are built, making the destination all the sweeter when we finally get there. We must lift Christ up in all we do and remain focused by fixing our eyes upon the goal of knowing Him. And we must never, ever give up or lose heart in our well-doing (see Galatians 6:9).

I have learned that waiting on God does not mean doing nothing. We cannot wait for life to happen, or it will pass us by. Who says I have to have a recording contract to record an album? Who says I have to live in Nashville to make it in the music business? Who says I have to have a degree in theory and composition before I can write a song?

Why do we listen to others when God's opinion is the one we need to be paying attention to? You can have all the visions in the world but see none of them come to pass if you do nothing about them. You will reap what you sow. Sow the visions of your heart on the soil of your resources and abilities, and then trust God to make them grow to maturity.

God is a big God, so dream big! Dreams can be simple or complex. In dreaming and achieving our goals, it is vital that we always remember who and whose we are. What others see on the outside should merely be a reflection of what is taking place on the inside of our hearts. We always have a choice as to how we respond to life, and life is better enjoyed by dreaming and heading toward the goal set before us: that of knowing Christ on an intimate level.

What are some of the dreams and goals that have shaped my life?

You know them by now. The goal of having my life and mind so transformed that what was once homosexual is now heterosexual. The goal of overcoming my bitterness toward those who have used me. The goal of seeing despair turned to joy, impatience to patience, harshness to gentleness, anger to peace, worry to trust.

Husband. Father. Musician. Author. Minister. Dreamer. Visionary. So many goals...and eternity to see them come to pass.

———

Truthstone
Luke 18:1-8
2 Corinthians 4:8-10
Hebrews 11

A Look Inside
1. What are my plans for those times when my dreams or visions come under attack?
2. Where will I go for strength when I am weary from waiting to see my dreams come to pass?
3. What will I do if God changes my course?

"Even in Their Sleep..."
Tonight, allow the Holy Spirit to give you a picture of your completed visions.

J-E-S-U-S

Listen, I will tell you 'bout the name of the King
Listen very carefully, do
He is my righteousness, Redeemer
He's the Lamb who was slain
He calls Himself Jehovah Tsidkenu

Mary had a little Lamb
And Jesus was His name
He came to set the sinners all free
The Lamb became a Shepherd
Always leading the way
He calls Himself Jehovah Rohi

Doctor! Doctor! We were headed for hell
All of us were dying in sin
Soon the Great Physician came to make us all well
Jehovah Rophe! Doctor is in!
Jehovah Rophe! Doctor is in!

PART
VIII

HEALING FOR
THE INJURED

The Purpose of Pain

I f you are reading this, you have probably been wounded deeply
in some way. Even if you don't *think* you have been wounded,
reality says something different. Sin leaves us all wounded. Whether
it is the devastation our own failure brings or the devastation we suffer at the hands of another, we have all been wounded in some way at
some time in our lives.

The reason I share this is because the Enemy would love to take
these hurts and use them to cause us to give up or give in to sin and
bitterness, both of which lead to the destruction of life and hope. God
allows us to go through the woundings of life so that we will grow. He
allows our injury in order to glorify Himself. He allows it to show us
our need for Him and to help us realize that we really can trust Him,
no matter what.

We have learned that for every giant, there is a stone (or stones)
that will fell him. The giants that seem unbeatable to us have no
power compared to the power of God exercised through us by His
Holy Spirit. And yet our battles with these giants are real, and they
leave real wounds in our souls.

Whether we like it or not, no one is immune to hurts or wounds.
Some are better than others at hiding their wounds. But even hidden
wounds take a toll upon our quality of life. Even if we hide those emotional or even physical wounds, we are all wounded by sin (see
Romans 3:23—"all have sinned and fall short of the glory of God").

Sin leaves emotional, mental, and spiritual wounds that even affect our physical bodies.

Sin affects our bodies and souls? Of course it does! How often do we allow our guilt and shame to make us emotional wrecks? How often do we allow unresolved issues to weaken our physical strength and make us susceptible to all manner of illness? Psalm 38:3 says, "Because of your wrath there is no health in my body; my bones have no soundness because of my sin."

In 3 John 2 we read John's greeting, "Dear friend, I pray that you may enjoy good health and that all may go well with you, even as your soul is getting along well."

The wounds of my life, left by the giants I have had to face, have set me on many journeys with the Lord that have led to deep levels of healing I never thought possible. Many times along the way I wished God would just zap me and heal me instantly. What I did not fully understand at the time was that sometimes the process is more important than the result because of the wisdom we gain.

The reason I feel compelled to write about my adventures in healing comes out of an incident that occurred on the night of August 10, 2000.

My friend Brent came over to play basketball with me. Having already schooled him thoroughly in a couple of games of Twenty-one, I agreed to play one more game with him. As the game neared its end (with me leading, of course), I made an awesome cut toward the basket with nothing but net in mind…when I suddenly heard a loud popping noise and felt tremendous pain in my left foot.

Hobbling over to the sideline, I spent a few minutes sitting and letting the pain subside before I laced my shoe back up and finished the game—which I lost, because I should have listened to the pain and not played in the first place.

The next morning, x-rays revealed a broken cuboid bone in my left foot. Dr. Weaver's first words were, "Well, let's cast it." At those words, I became emotional, remembering all I had gone through with my previous wound (the meeting between my left leg and a box blade that you will hear more about later) and could not imagine spending more time unable to get around freely. I begged the doctor to let me use the walking cast I had worn for five months during my previous injury. He said we could try it for a week. I am glad to report the next week's x-rays revealed that a good healing had begun, so I did not need to have a hard cast put on.

God immediately began using this episode to teach me more about Himself. But it had taken quite a lot of pain to get me to that place. When I first hurt my foot, my pride and my desire to finish the game caused me to ignore the pain. In a sense, I placed my mind in denial because I didn't want to appear weak and because I love to play the game so much. Either way, I ignored the signal—my pain—that something was wrong.

Often we try to disguise our pain or pretend it doesn't exist, because to acknowledge it would mean weakness (at least that's what a prideful response would be). Actually, I have found the opposite to be true.

The strongest I have ever felt is when I have humbled myself and admitted my weakness. For it is only then that I am in a position to receive help. Otherwise, if I played on without acknowledging my need, the time would come when my physical body would fail, and I would be forced to get help or to wallow in my woundedness. In either case, how could I receive help if I didn't acknowledge the pain?

How often do we take matters of the soul into our own hands when these matters would be better helped by a physician? What if you went to your doctor because you had a life-threatening wound, but would not let him look at your wound for fear of what others might think? That would be stupid. Yet how often do we say similar things to the Lord concerning the condition of our souls, turning away because the admission of failure—the admission that we have a wound—would be embarrassing?

If we never told our physician where we were hurting or never let him have a look, he could not help us. So it is with the Great Physician, Jesus Christ.

In order for healing to occur in our souls, we must first be honest with ourselves and admit that we have a need. We must then be honest with the Physician and show Him where it hurts. And once that hurt has been revealed, we must submit our souls to the One who can help us. If surgery is required, we must submit to that soul surgery. If a simple cleansing and binding of the wound is required, we must submit to that, whatever it is.

God's Word says that He "opposes the proud but gives grace [His strength] to the humble" (James 4:6). We must humbly learn to listen to the signals that pain sends us. If we do, we are on the road to healing already.

Truthstone
Psalm 103:1-5
Romans 3:23-25

A Look Inside
1. What is the pain in my life trying to tell me?
2. What are my wounds—and am I really willing to admit their existence to myself and to God?

"Even in Their Sleep…"
Ask God to help you better understand where you are hurting and how He wants to heal you.

THIRTY-
FOUR

The Process of Healing

O ne sunny September afternoon a few years ago, I decided to
take the box blade off my tractor. I had been using it to dredge
an area near my pond, but I needed to attach another implement to
the tractor so I could perform other tasks around the farm.

In case you did not grow up on a farm as I did, let me tell you
that a box blade is a formidable piece of equipment that weighs in at
around five hundred pounds. Five feet wide by two feet high, it is a
single piece of steel similar to what you would see on a road grader.
Attached to the part of the blade nearest the tractor are a series of two-
foot-long tines, called rippers, that break up the dirt, allowing the
blade to follow along and scoop up the dirt.

Typically, one would ask for help with such a large piece of equipment. But I had been doing farm work like this since I was a boy, so
I figured I could handle it. In my wisdom I decided that if I raised the
hydraulic arms just a few inches off the ground, I could then slide the
blade near enough to the edge of the arm to lower it to the ground
and slide it off.

My plan worked well—too well, in fact. Instead of the blade slid-
ing to the edge and stopping, as I had planned, its weight sent it off
the equipment's arm and onto my leg. One of the rippers lived up to
its name, ripping right through my calf. I was pinned between the
blade and the tractor wheel.

Once the initial shock wore off, I began to have thoughts about dying in this position. I imagined Melinda and our children wailing as they found my dead body. In my mind I saw my friends Matt, Brent, and Chuck shaking their heads at me for finding such a stupid way to die.

Finally, I cried out to the Lord to preserve my life, and He did. He gave me the strength to lift the blade from my leg and to hobble toward the house. Melinda came out of the house at just the right moment, spotted me, and rushed me to the emergency room.

Though no bones were broken, the flesh that had covered the wound died because it had been severed from its blood source. I assumed the physician would perform a skin graft to cover the gaping hole, but he informed me that this would not work. Such wounds must heal from the inside out, he said. I was told to pack the wound with sterile gauze every day, allowing the wound to bleed as much as possible because (in the doctor's words) "there is life in the blood."

Now, where had I heard about life being in the blood?

Telling the Israelites what they could and could not eat, God clearly forbade them to consume any animal's blood. "For the life of a creature is in the blood, and I have given it to you to make atonement for yourselves on the altar; it is the blood that makes atonement for one's life" (Leviticus 17:11). For us, likewise, "the blood of Jesus… purifies us from all sin" (1 John 1:7).

The blood of Jesus brought me spiritual life in the first place and remains a healing agent for my soul's wounds. But what is the packing material of my soul wounds? As I pondered this, the Lord reminded me that most of my wounds had come as the result of believing the lies of the Enemy. These types of wounds are healed from the inside out. The packing material? God's Word.

Whenever the Lord has me share my story of deliverance publicly, the giant of shame or the giant of the fear of rejection comes as a liar, trying to keep me from sharing hope with others in bondage. This sometimes opens up an old wound. But I am prepared because I have taken the time to pack that wounded place carefully.

So what have I packed there?

When the old wounds of my identity are thrown into my face by the Enemy, I pack that wound with Romans 6:1-2: "What shall we say, then? Shall we go on sinning so that grace may increase? By no means! We died to sin; how can we live in it any longer?"

When I stumble and fall and the Enemy condemns me and tries to persuade me to forsake the ground I have gained, I pack Micah 7:8 into that wound.

> Do not gloat over me, my enemy!
>   Though I have fallen, I will rise.
> Though I sit in darkness,
>   the LORD will be my light.

Whenever old wounds are opened up by the Enemy, I pull out the truth of God's Word that I have packed there, and with that packing material comes out all the deadness from my old life that no longer defines me. Lies are exposed and truth once again prevails over the wounded places in my life. After a while, the Enemy stops attacking those places, because the infection of sin has at last been cured.

Going through the process of healing from the injury to my calf was not always pleasant, and it was certainly not brief. But it *was* necessary. So it is with my soul. So it shall be with yours.

Learn to pack God's Word into your soul and pull it out as often as needed. What may seem painful soon becomes a place of healing. You can enjoy new life with a sense of joy and the strength of wisdom gained along the way.

———

Truthstone
Jeremiah 17:14
Romans 6:1-4

A Look Inside
1. What are some of the wounds I carry in my soul?
2. Where am I in the process of healing in each area of wounding?
3. What packing material from God's Word do I need to place there?

"Even in Their Sleep…"
Ask the Lord to help you meditate on and memorize a certain scripture that can be packed into your wounded place.

THIRTY-FIVE

Battle Scars

W hen I was about five years old, I went into the pasture to pet our horse, Big Red. Big Red was appropriately named—he stood sixteen hands tall and towered above my little self. On this particular day I am recalling, Big Red decided he needed a taste of me, and he began to bite me. So I did what any five-year-old in such a spot would do: I ran. Big Red ran after me.

Trying to escape, I climbed the mulberry tree that had grown into the fence line of Big Red's pasture. But Big Red, being big, could still reach me. And he still seemed in the mood for a nibble of young Dennis. So next I jumped out of the tree…and found myself straddling the barbed-wire fence.

After I received the stitches required to repair my wound, my first response was, "I can't wait to show everyone!" The scar left by this wound became a badge of honor for me with the other guys. It served as a reminder to me and to anyone else who cared to see it that I was pretty cool.

I still bear that three-inch scar on my right leg, along with a number of others I have accumulated in accidents over the years. And over those years I've done a lot of thinking about scars. What they say about our past. What they say about our present and our future.

Dealing with giants never leaves us untouched. When we go into battle, we inevitably endure wounds. And when our wounds heal, scars naturally form. They mark the place where at one time we sustained an injury. But they also mark the places where God has healed us. They say that the time of injury—this injury, at least—is over.

Jesus did battle for us on the cross, and He bore the scars from it. His brow pocked by the points of thorns, His hands and feet pierced by nails, His side torn by a spear—these bear the marks of His struggle against Satan for the souls of sinners. His scars remind us of the healing work accomplished in and through Him. Jesus's scars have inspired me to expose the scars of my past as a means of helping others find the same hope and healing I have found.

In my case, I carry with me the scar of homosexuality. Healed? Indeed. But instead of cowering in fear that someone might find out, I decided to expose the scar in the hope that others who suffer the same wounding might realize that healing is possible. A scar is nothing to be ashamed of, and as with the wounding itself, it takes on a whole new meaning when viewed from God's perspective.

So how do we view scars? For me, a scar can either be a sign that says, "Look what God has done," or a shadow that lurks under cover in my life. It can be a trophy of glory I proudly display or a point of shame I try to hide.

Do you hide your scars, or do you let others see them?

Some people prefer to hide a scar. They are ashamed of what it says about their past. Furthermore, they think that if others know they bear such a scar, these people won't accept them any longer. Bad reasoning.

Our choice to hide our scars is bad for us and bad for others. As we keep our injuries hidden, we inhibit the fullest possible flow of life and hinder healing because that area is blocked off and set off-limits. Not exposing our scars also prevents others who have been injured from benefiting from our example of healing.

What if I had chosen never to tell anyone about my past involvement in homosexuality? What if I had never testified to God's grace in setting me free from this sin? I'll tell you what. Countless numbers of people with the same kind of wounding, as well as other kinds of wounding from sin, would never have been ministered to by my testimony.

If I had not been honest about my sin, I would never have been healed. In the same way, if I am not honest about what my scars mean, they become a hindrance rather than a sign of healing and, yes, even of beauty!

When I was a child, my scars seemed enormous to me. But as an adult I have a different perspective. My scars haven't grown, but I have. Now I am able to give God thanks in the midst of the wounding because I know that any scars I incur will ultimately become badges of honor that say, "Look what God has done here!" My scars are evidence of His mercy and grace and love in my life.

Truthstone
Isaiah 53
John 20:24-29

A Look Inside
1. What scars from my past serve as reminders of God's healing in my life?
2. If I were to look at my scars from the Lord's perspective, how might I see them differently?
3. How can God receive glory from the scars of my life?

"Even in Their Sleep…"
Ask the Holy Spirit to give you a glimpse of the scars of your life from His perspective, and then meditate on how He might desire to bring glory to Christ through them.

Conclusion

If you had told me twenty-five years ago that one day I would be free from homosexuality and that God would have me share the most shameful parts of my past for His glory, I would have thought you were crazy. But that is exactly what God has done. How does such healing come? How are giants slain in our lives once and for all?

To slay a giant, we must not only knock him senseless with a stone; we must also cut off his head. And since all evil giants are based upon deceit in one way or another, we cut off a giant's head with a mighty swing from the sword of God's truth. We do this by listening to who God says we are, not to the lies of our past experiences or temptations.

With the power of God's truth, you *can* destroy the giant in your life. An addiction? You can overcome it. Habitual sin? You can break the habit. Fear, doubt, or anxiety? You can become spiritually and emotionally whole. Remember, however, that giants are not necessarily slain in an instant.

Here the image of a stronghold may be more helpful. It may take a long time to build a stronghold, and it may take an equal length of time to tear it down. After years of habitually believing the lies of the Enemy about ourselves, it will take awhile to tear down those lies and start believing the truth of what God says about us. What I have found, though, is that getting honest with God and others leads to moments of God's graciously speeding up the process. Truth can often be like a shot of vitamin B12 to the weakened body of an athlete. It invigorates the soul and helps him keep running the race, no matter how long or how grueling the race is.

Remember, also, that giants are best faced one at a time. I didn't go after fear, rejection, discouragement, and perversion all on the same day. I made the initial commitment to be a giant slayer facing that first battle "alone" with God. But all the giants I have slain since that day, I have not faced alone. Like David, I have surrounded myself with many mighty men and women of valor who have fought the fight with me as the right time has come.

Ultimately, I had to *want* to slay the giants, and then I had to realize that I could not keep my eyes on me and slay them. My purpose in this life is not to receive glory and riches or to have endless pleasures. My purpose is to seek God's glory and His pleasure and to see others come to know Him as I have. Put simply, it's not about me. Healing comes as I focus on God and others.

My sin may seem like a mountain, but in reality—that is, in comparison to God—my sin is more like a speed bump, while God's love, power, and presence are like the grandeur of Mount Everest. I must learn to *glance* at my problems and *gaze* upon His greatness. I must learn to accept my weakness and embrace His saving grace on a moment-by-moment basis. I must learn to hear His voice and rely on the power of His precious Holy Spirit. I must be about my Father's business.

After years of fighting giants, there are some things I know: Truth is the foundation I must build my identity upon. Contentment comes from knowing that God is in control regardless of my temptations or circumstances. Temptation does not equal my identity but rather is an opportunity to be more intimate with my God. I do not get to decide if God loves me or likes me—God *is* love, and my only choice is to accept or reject His love for me. Bottom line? I am who my Father says I am, regardless of my past sin or present failure or temptation.

Wrong thoughts lead to wrong behavior. Wrong behavior leads to crippling habits. Crippling habits lead to bondage and death and giants to rule over our lives. Giants are in the business of cutting off the relationship between us and God.

Are you tired of the giants called shame, discouragement, fear, evil desires, and sin that leave you cold and alone? Then take your place as a giant killer. Take up the stone of identity in Christ and slay shame once and for all. Take up the stone of divine perspective and see the grand vista God has intended for you all along. Take up the stone of intimacy with God and walk in levels of relational freedom you never thought possible in this life. Take up the stone of praise and worship and watch God bring peace to the greatest storms and darkest nights of your life. Take up the stone of dreams for the future and walk in your identity as a son or daughter of the Most High God.

Become the giant killer God intends you to be and walk in the company of the likes of King David and his mighty men. Become a giant killer and follow the greatest Giant Killer of all—the One who conquered sin, death, shame, fear, rejection, evil desires, and all manner of perversions once and for all. *The* Giant Killer, Jesus Christ.

My Frequently Asked Questions

1. Is There Really Anything Wrong with Homosexuality?

Homosexuality is a perversion, a deviation from what is normal. What-ever influences—biology or upbringing—might have moved a person toward homosexuality, it is just not true that being homosexual is either inevitable or acceptable. After having lived in that perversion, and after having believed that was "just the way I was born," I am now able to truthfully say that God can change the heart and mind of the homosexual.

I have no doubt now that heterosexuality is right and that homo-sexuality is wrong for every one of us. Why is that? Because God ordained it so. One can look at the female body and at the male body and see they were meant for each other. Homosexuality is obviously unnatural.

Furthermore, God's Word is clear concerning the fact that it is sin-ful for either men or women to have sexual relations with members of the same sex (see Leviticus 18:22; 20:13; Romans 1:26-27; 1 Corinthi-ans 6:9-10; 1 Timothy 1:9-10). Homosexuals interested in Christian-ity have had to re-create God in their own image in order to try to squelch the shame and guilt of their perversity. I've been there. I know.

I do not believe that gay people are born gay; they are just born sinful—like everyone else. Though it may seem to them that they could never be anything other than homosexual, that does not excuse them. Other sexual deviants—the rapist, the child molester, and so on—could also claim, "This is the way I was born; I can't help myself." No one would therefore say that we should accept and affirm the child molester. Yet that is the sort of thing that people who are homosexually deviant are asking us to do in their case.

God desires life—abundant life—for His children. I find it interesting that a perversion of God's best (a healthy sexual relationship between a man and a woman) cannot naturally bring forth life. The homosexual cannot, by natural means, bring forth life but must instead artificially engineer it or recruit others for this purpose. And the best recruiter for the cause of perversion is Satan, the liar.

In 1 Corinthians 6:9-11 the apostle Paul gave an account of sins God can heal, including homosexuality. He said to his original readers, "That is what some of you were" (verse 11). In other words, even then homosexuality was a sin problem—a sin problem that could be overcome. Homosexuals will often claim that they were born that way, but I can tell you that God has made a way for them to be *re*born, spiritually speaking, and to become heterosexual. By placing their faith in Christ, they can have their identities totally transformed.

My stance on this issue may seem harsh, but that is not my intention. It is out of the life-changing power of God's love that I share so boldly. I want others to know the freedom I have found. Change can come when we admit to ourselves and to God that we need it. We must agree with God that He is our Maker. Otherwise, we will stay where we are.

2. Was Your Healing from Homosexuality Instantaneous, or Was It a Process?

In a word, yes!

I believe that when I became a new creation, my core identity was transformed forever. On November 7, 1981, I walked away from the homosexual lifestyle and chose to follow after God and whatever He had for me, no matter what. In other words, who I really am was sealed in an instant on that night so long ago.

But my healing has also been a process. It took me years to build up the identity of homosexuality in my life, whether or not I consciously knew what I was doing. (Just because I didn't realize I was making a choice did not make it any less of a choice.) My belief is that if it took years to build up that old identity, it would probably take years to tear it down and rebuild God's destiny for me and my identity.

My life has been a journey of walking with God in an intimate way. As we walk together, He faithfully reminds me when I am letting the old ways determine my identity. Just as no temptation defines me, neither do my past experiences or old sinful memories. No longer do I allow outward things to determine my inner reality. Who I am is determined only by my Father. I am who He says I am.

Has my journey been easy? No way. Has it been worth every struggle against my old life? You bet!

3. Are You Still Tempted by Homosexuality?

Yes, but not in the same manner. So much freedom has come to my life in the past twenty years that I can honestly say that even if someone approached me with a proposition for homosexual activity, such a proposition would have no effect on me. I would respond with an ill feeling or with laughter.

Do I remember what those experiences from my past felt like? Yes. But those feelings do not equate to temptation. They are simply part of the consequences of my sin. They spark a memory, but they do not lead to sin, because I have learned a better way and seek the God-given way of escape (see 1 Corinthians 10:13).

For me, the way of escape has meant many things. Initially, that way of escape was to cut off all relationships from my homosexual past. (Does that sound unloving to you? Get over it. I was no one's savior. Only Jesus could fit that bill for me or my former friends.)

Furthermore, the way of escape meant that I needed to rid my life of any mementos from my old life: pictures, gifts, clothing, and so on. If these items were still around, they would serve as reminders of past failures and could possibly lead to further downfall.

I found another great way of escape was to stop going to places where temptation might occur. I learned to put myself in the best possible place for victory rather than set myself up for defeat. The way of escape came as I sought intimacy with Jesus whenever I was tempted. (The sheer number of songs I have received over the years stands as a testament to God's delivering power in moments of weakness.)

4. Did Leaving Homosexuality Mean Denying Your Emotional Nature?

To be highly emotional is often considered a feminine trait. And it is true that I have always been quite emotional and that this played a part in my identifying myself as homosexual. What I have had to learn is that emotions are not necessarily bad. They can, in fact, be very good.

Emotional sensitivity is a gift from the Lord. Everyone has a measure of feelings. I just happen to have more emotional sensitivity than many men do, and that is how God wanted me to be. It is a good thing.

On the other hand, since emotions are a gift I have been given, I am responsible for handling them properly. I have had to learn how to use those emotions in a holy way. That is, I must use them in a way that is in keeping with God's truth.

Just because I perceive that someone has rejected me (whether the rejection is real or imagined) doesn't mean I have to give in to feelings of rejection. Those feelings lead to unholy behavior. The truth is that God loves me and does not reject me. He will not leave me. He will not forsake me.

Feelings of acceptance lead to holy behavior. Rather than withdrawing from others, I now seek out others whom I sense feel rejection, and I minister acceptance to them. Rather than becoming bitter toward those who reject me, I now choose to forgive them and to minister blessings to them. Rather than disregard the feelings of others, I now become even more sensitive to the needs of others and to minister as the Spirit leads.

A right belief systems leads to right feelings.

Emotions can be giants in our lives, but when we slay their improper use, we have the ability to raise them up as *holy* giants that help us battle the other giants in our lives.

5. Do You Consider Yourself a "Recovering Homosexual"?

For me to say I am a "recovering homosexual" would mean that, in some capacity, I am still homosexual. To me, that is not victory. If I have been saved and reborn, then the reality of who I am—the core of my identity—is forever changed. This means that, like Lazarus who was called forth from the dead but was still wrapped in all those grave clothes, I am as alive in my new identity as I can be. I just need to strip away the old outward stuff that I thought defined me.

When Jesus confronted the crowd who wished to stone the woman who had been caught in an adulterous affair, He told them to let the one who was without sin cast the first stone. That was an awesome statement, but the most important part of that encounter, to me, was when He told the woman, "Go now and leave your life of sin" (John 8:11).

Did the woman suddenly cease remembering her adulterous life? No. Did she stop missing the one she had the affair with? Probably not right away. Was she still haunted by the memories and reminders of who she had been? Of course. Was she still tempted to believe that she was born to be sexually promiscuous? I am sure she was. But did the forgiving power of Jesus and her newfound identity as one who would go and sin no more give her the grace to overcome all her past and all the wrong perceptions concerning her identity? I believe they did.

Like that woman, I chose to go and sin no more—in my case, to sin no more in the homosexual arena. Homosexuality is not my identity, regardless of whether I ever experienced it or am ever tempted by it. Since it is a learned perception, it can be unlearned and replaced by something better. I chose to believe God and to stop believing the Enemy's lies about who I am. If I am truly born again, then the old homosexual Dennis has been put to death and a new heterosexual Dennis has been raised to new life.

6. How Can I Minister to Someone Who Is Struggling with Same-Sex Attractions?

God commands us to love. Love requires action. As John 3:16 states, "For God so loved the world that He *gave…*" (emphasis added). Who did Jesus spend time with? With the outcasts of society. In many ways homosexuals already feel like outcasts, and in most cases they have experienced rejection early in life. We must learn to love without condemning the person. We must learn to love those in bondage without embracing the lies behind their bondage. The bottom line in ministering to homosexuals (or to anyone in *any* kind of bondage) is to be willing to walk toward Jesus with them.

A friend of mine told me, "I don't know all the answers, but I do know *the* answer: Jesus. And I'm willing to walk toward Him with you, no matter how long it takes. No matter how difficult the journey." The main way you can minister to someone is to be willing to walk toward Jesus with him. This demonstrates love just as Jesus demonstrated His love for us even though we did not deserve it. When we commit to walk toward Jesus with someone, we must be willing to speak the truth when the lies raise their giant heads. We must be willing to help him back to his feet when he stumbles and falls. We must be willing to love him in spite of the setbacks. We must be willing to serve him as Jesus came to serve us. We must be there to cheer him on in the race he is running.

Some ways you might be able to help? People who want out of homosexuality need to know someone is there for them. It is very important that the fear of rejection be dealt with. In other words, help them put down the giant of fear of rejection by recognizing their lack of trust. How? By simply being there for them. Often, acting as a sounding board can be the most beneficial thing you can do to help someone walk out of bondage. I myself have experienced much healing by simply talking myself into the truth.

Practically speaking, walking out of bondage with someone is beneficial to both parties. As we walk together toward Jesus, we often find freedom in areas of our lives in which we never realized we were in bondage! Be willing to humble yourself right along with the struggler you are seeking to help. Humility goes a long way in gaining someone else's trust.

Be a servant to those who are struggling. Jesus laid down His life for others; we are to do the same. Often, we let our reluctance to be inconvenienced overshadow the opportunity to help someone. My wife, Melinda, and I have seen many people come to freedom simply because we didn't allow inconveniences to keep us from ministering to a hurting soul. We have been awakened at all hours of the night. We have opened our home to emotionally wounded people and have included our own children in the ministry. Serving others in ministry may simply mean spending time with them as you would spend time with your own family. Seeing how a healthy family operates can give strugglers a vision for health in their own lives and relationships.

As you seek to minister to those who are struggling with homosexuality, it is important that you research the issue thoroughly and gather resources that will equip you to help. By becoming familiar with the resources, you can also make them available to strugglers, encouraging them to apply the truths they discover to their own lives.

In my own walk out of bondage, I entrusted my soul to many people along the way. If not for those God placed in my life during this time, my journey would have been lonely and much more difficult. When I cried, they provided a shoulder to lean on. When I repeated the same patterns of believing certain lies over and over again, they did not bang their heads against the wall in frustration. Instead, they became a rock I could turn to again and again to hear the truth until my shackles finally broke and I could receive and apply that truth victoriously to my own life.

When I became confused about the focus or direction of my life, these faithful ministers acted as beacons of hope, helping me discern God's best for me. When I became weary in running the race, they were there to cheer me on and provide life-giving drinks from the resources of their own wells of faith. When I needed godly role models, they showed me how a man should act or treat others and how a man should seek hard after God. Just as David surrounded himself with mighty men to help him through the battles of life, so too are we to surround ourselves with such men—and women! And after we're set free, we are to then turn around and begin surrounding others who are in need of rescue, becoming mighty men and women who fight for their freedom!

You do not have to have struggled with homosexuality yourself to help someone else. You simply have to know Jesus. You must also remember that you are not the Savior. Jesus is. The people you are trying to help are always responsible for their own choices. You cannot choose for anyone else. Love the person. Pray for the person. Just be available. Be a mighty man (or woman) of valor who fights for freedom in the lives of those in bondage.

7. What Resources Would You Recommend Either for Those Struggling with Homosexuality or for Those Who Want to Minister to Homosexuals?

Because of the nature of my story, I have the honor of sharing my testimony around the country. My hope is that others would see that freedom is truly possible. The only problem with sharing that story is that those who desire freedom either for themselves or for a loved one want to talk with me personally in the hope that I might be able to help them through their journey. If I were able to fulfill each of these requests, I would spend 24 hours a day, 7 days a week, 365 days a year doing just that! The reality is that it is simply not physically possible. But do not despair. God has raised up many resources to help answer your questions and guide you through your own journey toward defeating the giants that war against your identity or the identity of a friend or loved one. Following are some of my favorite resources:

Books

Dallas, Joe. *Desires in Conflict: Hope for Men Who Struggle with Sexual Identity.* Rev. ed. Eugene, OR: Harvest House, 2003.

———. *A Strong Delusion: Confronting the "Gay Christian" Movement.* Eugene, OR: Harvest House, 1996.

———. *Unforgiven Sins.* Eugene, OR: Harvest House, 1995.

Worthen, Anita, and Bob Davies. *Someone I Love Is Gay: How Family and Friends Can Respond.* Downers Grove, IL: InterVarsity Press, 1996.

Organizations, Ministries, and Conferences

Cross Ministry, Inc.
PO Box 1122
Wake Forest, NC 27588
919-569-0375
www.crossministry.org

Desert Stream Ministries/Living Waters
PO Box 17635
Anaheim, CA 92817-7635
714-779-6899
E-mail: info@desertstream.org
www.desertstream.org

Exchanged Life Ministries Texas
9560 Skillman
Suite 124
Dallas, TX 75243
972-680-8541
E-mail: elm@exchangedlife.org
www.exchangedlife.org

Exodus International
PO Box 540119
Orlando, FL 32854
888-264-0877
www.exodus-international.org or http://exodus.to
www.exodusnorthamerica.org

Love Won Out—A one-day conference on understanding and
    addressing homosexuality
Focus on the Family
800-232-6459
www.lovewonout.com

More Than Words—A one-day conference on understanding
    homosexuality
Cross Ministry, Inc.
PO Box 1122

Wake Forest, NC 27588
919-569-0375
www.crossministry.org

Regeneration Books—A ministry of Exodus International
PO Box 540119
Orlando, FL 32854
www.regenbooks.org

Other Resources
Genesis Counseling/Joe Dallas
17632 Irvine Blvd., Suite 220
Tustin, CA 92869
714-502-1463
www.genesiscounseling.org
Joe Dallas is the founder of Genesis Counseling, a former gay-rights
activist, and a former staff member of a Metropolitan Commu-
nity Church. He has helped hundreds of men and women who
struggle with homosexuality and related problems. He is available for conferences and seminars.

The Real Truth About Homosexuality—Provides a scientific and
biblical perspective on what homosexuality is and is not
www.therealtruthabouthomosexuality.com

To learn more about WaterBrook Press and view
our catalog of products, log on to our Web site:
www.waterbrookpress.com

WATERBROOK
PRESS